FOR THE ULTIMATE FAN

DUDEPERFECT

101 TRICKS, TIPS, -AND- *COOL STUFF*

dp | **DUDE**PERFECT

with TRAVIS THRASHER

Thomas Nelson®
Since 1798
thomasnelson.com

Dude Perfect 101 Tricks, Tips, and Cool Stuff

Copyright © 2021 by Tyler Toney, Coby Cotton, Cory Cotton, Cody Jones, and Garrett Hilbert

Tommy Nelson, PO Box 141000, Nashville, TN 37214

Published in Nashville, Tennessee, by Tommy Nelson. Tommy Nelson is an imprint of Thomas Nelson. Thomas Nelson is a registered trademark of HarperCollins Christian Publishing, Inc.

Authors are represented by the literary agency of The Fedd Agency, Inc., P.O. Box 341973, Austin, Texas 78734.

Tommy Nelson titles may be purchased in bulk for educational, business, fund-raising, or sales promotional use. For information, please e-mail SpecialMarkets@ThomasNelson.com.

Note to parents: This book contains a number of activities which may be dangerous if not done exactly as directed or which may be inappropriate for young children. All of these activities should be carried out under adult supervision. The authors and publisher expressly disclaim liability for any injury or damages that result from engaging in the activities contained in this book.

Library of Congress Cataloging-in-Publication Data

Names: Dude Perfect (Group), author. | Thrasher, Travis, 1971- author.
Title: Dude Perfect 101 tricks, tips, and cool stuff / Dude Perfect with Travis Thrasher.
Description: Nashville, TN : Thomas Nelson, [2021] | Includes bibliographical references.
| Audience: Ages 8-12 | Summary: "From trick shots to mind-bending stunts to setting absurd records, Dude Perfect 101 Tricks, Tips, and Cool Stuff offers a full-color, at-home, screen-free adventure for young people eager to accept the challenge of performing the same unbelievable maneuvers that has made Dude Perfect a cultural phenomenon"-- Provided by publisher.
Identifiers: LCCN 2020054859 (print) | LCCN 2020054860 (ebook) | ISBN 9781400217076 (hardcover) | ISBN 9781400217090 (epub)
Subjects: LCSH: Dude Perfect (Group)--Biography--Juvenile literature. |
Dude Perfect (Group)--Biography. sears | Tricks--Juvenile literature. |
Sports--Juvenile literature.
Classification: LCC GV1548 .D84 2021 (print) | LCC GV1548 (ebook) | DDC
    793.8--dc23
LC record available at https://lccn.loc.gov/2020054859
LC ebook record available at https://lccn.loc.gov/2020054860

ISBN 978-1-4002-1709-0 (Ebook)
ISBN 978-1-4002-1707-6 (Hardcover)

Written by *Dude Perfect with Travis Thrasher*
Illustrated by *Diego Vaisberg and Martin Lowenstein at DGPH Studio*
Photography: *Images used with permission from Dude Perfect*
Art direction: *Sabryna Lugge*
Interior design: *Kathy Mitchell, Kathy Mitchell Design*

Printed in the United States

21 22 23 24 25 PC/LSCW 10 9 8 7 6 5

This book is for everyone who has watched one of our videos at full volume—or low volume—and still chose to watch another one. Thank you for supporting us in our crazy dream to entertain. Thank you for following along every step of the way and for letting us share our memories with you. In a world filled with negativity, you've given us overwhelming encouragement over the last twelve years. Thank you for that. Thank you for everything. We believe the best is yet to come.

GOD BLESS!

CONTENTS

WELCOME!

IT WAS THE SEASON OF SWISHES and the dawning of dunks. It was crazy stunts, epic fun, and world record baskets. It was a water bottle flip, having fun with stereotypes, and the wrath of the Rage Monster. It was the age of all-sports battles and the era of overtime. It was wild.

It was . . . awesome.

And really, it still is. Because first and foremost, we're friends.

Dude Perfect started as exactly that, a group of friends from school: the twins with the bowl-cuts, the tall goofy jock, the clean freak, and the crazy, bearded guy. And of course, later, one magical day, we found Panda. On paper, none of this should work—and we say "paper" because this is *literally* paper you're reading. But anyway, we just clicked. And like the videos we're making, we're still clicking—and so are you, hopefully, if you're reading this book. (Yeah, that's a clicking pun, and we love puns, especially Coby.)

In 2007 we made a backyard trickshot video—purely for fun—and it went viral. That was the start, and as we graduated college it led to the scary decision to quit our jobs and keep running with this whole Dude Perfect thing. We were all in from the start—having no idea what Dude Perfect would grow into—or all the laughs that lay ahead of us.

One thing we absolutely know: we have *the best* fans in the world. We love that we have supporters from all ages and backgrounds, from all around the world. And we're proud to know that families watch our videos together. We care about each person who watches our videos, and we consider them our friends. And that includes *you* if you're reading this now. (Special shout out to each of our subscribers—currently over fifty-five million—you guys have a special place in our hearts.)

One of the cool things about having fans like you following our lives on camera is that you guys—essentially—hang out with us a lot. That said, we thought it would be super fun to make a book that helps us hang out a little differently. If you've ever wanted to do what we do, see how we do it, and have a blast in the process, you're in the right place. The following pages are filled with all kinds of fun things to teach you more about us and help you do what we do. We've shared **101 trick shots** for you to try at home, along with dozens of tips and cool stuff.

As far as the stunts go, we're not gonna lie—a lot of these tricks will require faith, patience, dedication, practice, and teamwork. Throughout the book, you'll see three main categories: Tricks, Tips, and Cool Stuff.

TRICKS
Tricks are fun trick shots, stunts, and battles we want *you* to try yourself. Don't worry—we'll tell you what to do. Remember, this is what it's all about, and it's how we got started in the first place!

TIPS
In addition to providing step-by-step instructions for some of our bigger tricks, we offer helpful tips throughout. These tips will help you do what we do, with suggestions we've never shared before.

COOL STUFF
Cool Stuff will be crazy-fun, behind-the-scenes facts and info about us five goofballs. We might regret sharing these details because some are pretty embarrassing. But unfortunately, it's too late—they're already permanently inked into this book. We also include a lot of the science behind the tricks and fun facts to offer deeper insight into how they work.

In short, think of this as the super-fun, know-it-all guide to Dude Perfect. We worked hard to put a *lot* of goodness in here, so let's get started. In fact, let's kick this thing off the right way:

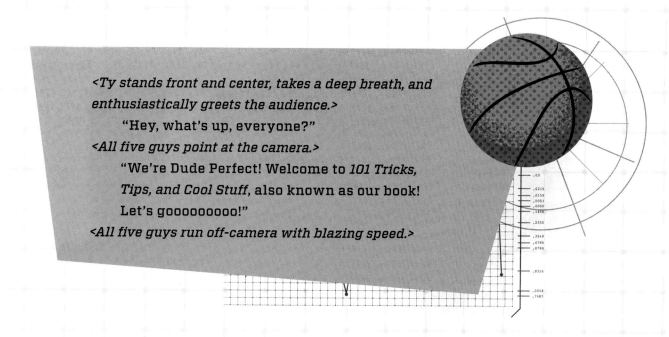

<Ty stands front and center, takes a deep breath, and enthusiastically greets the audience.>

"Hey, what's up, everyone?"

<All five guys point at the camera.>

"We're Dude Perfect! Welcome to *101 Tricks, Tips, and Cool Stuff*, also known as our book! Let's gooooooooo!"

<All five guys run off-camera with blazing speed.>

INTRODUCING

TYLER TONEY

1   **One word to describe yourself:** Unpredictable.

2   **An interesting fact about yourself:** I know who the Panda is.

3   **Another interesting fact:** I hold the unofficial world record as the only person to hit 50 million subscribers on their birthday.

4   **Favorite video you've ever made:** "Airsoft Battle Royale."

5   **Favorite trick you've done:** Airplane shot, Cowboys stadium shot, world's longest archery shot.

6   **Craziest thing you've ever done in a video:** Getting slapped in the face by Dale Earnhardt Jr.

7   **If you weren't in Dude Perfect, you'd be:** Hosting my own hunting and fishing show.

8   **One trick or shot you'd like to do:** The first trick shot on the moon.

9   **Favorite sport:** Football, hockey, Wiffle ball, and fishing—in no particular order.

10   **When you're not making videos, you're . . . :** Being a husband to Bethany, and being a dad to Barrett, Colton, and Rhett. And spending time outdoors with family and close friends.

11   **Life motto or personal tagline:** "The field may be long, the ceiling may be short, but the game goes on forever."

INTRODUCING
GARRETT HILBERT

1	**One word to describe yourself:** Purple.
2	**An interesting fact about yourself:** I have a master's degree in architecture.
3	**Another interesting fact:** I'm obsessive when it comes to being clean.
4	**Favorite video you've ever made:** Filming with Chris Paul and Aaron Rodgers for a trick shot video.
5	**Favorite trick you've done:** Making a shot out of a blimp.
6	**Craziest thing you've ever done in a video:** In "Real Life Trick Shots," I threw a video game disc from about eight feet away and landed it in the disc slot of the game system.
7	**If you weren't in Dude Perfect, you'd be:** Hopefully employed at a world-class architectural firm designing buildings.
8	**One trick or shot you'd like to do:** Film with Tiger Woods at the Masters Tournament in Augusta, Georgia: He steps up on number 12 and holes out. Then I step up and hole out, and then we celebrate together.
9	**Favorite sport:** To play, soccer. To watch, football and soccer.
10	**When you're not making videos, you're . . . :** Being a husband and being a dad to my three kids, watching sports, and hanging with friends.
11	**Life motto or personal tagline:** "Trick shots are forever, bro." Or "I live in reality, and I know I'm good."

COBY COTTON

1	**One word to describe yourself:** WINNER!
2	**An interesting fact about yourself:** I can sleep anywhere—like on concrete—no problem.
3	**Another interesting fact:** Cory will tell you I broke his arm in seventh grade, but I would say that he tripped and fell.
4	**Favorite video you've ever made:** "Pickup Basketball Stereotypes."
5	**Favorite trick you've done:** Paper Shredder from "Real Life Trick Shots."
6	**Craziest thing you've ever done in a video:** Lying in the coffin with all those snakes.
7	**If you weren't in Dude Perfect, you'd be:** Dreaming up an invention for *Shark Tank*.
8	**One trick or shot you'd like to do:** Make a hole in one.
9	**Favorite sport:** Basketball.
10	**When you're not making videos, you're . . . :** Playing basketball, golf, or hanging with my awesome wife and daughter.
11	**Life motto or personal tagline:** "Chocolate milk forever!"

INTRODUCING

CORY COTTON

1	**One word to describe yourself:** Lucky.
2	**An interesting fact about yourself:** If you watch *Overtime*, you know the word above does *not* in fact describe my history on the worst game show ever: Wheel Unfortunate.
3	**Another interesting fact:** If a milkshake is on the menu, I order it 100 percent of the time. Nutella chocolate pretzel is my personal fave.
3.5	**And another interesting fact:** Coby broke my arm in seventh grade. While playing basketball, I got by him, jumped in the air toward the goal, and he pushed me from behind. These are the facts. He will likely deny this, but on the inside, he *knows* the truth.
4	**Favorite video you've ever made:** "Real Life Trick Shots" series and "Pickup Basketball Stereotypes."
5	**Favorite trick you've done:** Shooting a basketball through the net, off the bounce back, and into the one open spot on the ball rack was one of my shiniest moments. (Real talk: it took three days because it was #Hard #Commitment #ForTheFans.)
6	**Craziest thing you've ever done in a video:** Easy— getting my eyebrows shaved off. It *only* took two or three *months* of eyebrow growth before people stopped staring awkwardly at me.
7	**If you weren't in Dude Perfect, you'd be:** Working for Apple in marketing, or as a youth pastor.
8	**One trick or shot you'd like to do:** I'd still love to do a shot in the Grand Canyon.
9	**Favorite sport:** Basketball. All day.
10	**When you're not making videos, you're . . . :** Hanging with my family or playing basketball and golf. I have two-year-old twins (*strong* twin powers in the Cotton family) and a one-year-old baby boy.
11	**Life motto or personal tagline:** "Let's goooo!" Ideally you hold your arms out like an airplane while saying it. (My Team Cory fans know!)

CODY JONES

1	**One word to describe yourself:** Loud.
2	**An interesting fact about yourself:** I've dislocated my shoulder seven times.
3	**Another interesting fact:** I've been married for over ten years.
4	**Favorite video you've ever made:** Basketball World Records.
5	**Favorite trick you've done:** Blindfolded Full Court Basketball Shot. It was a first-try miracle!
6	**Craziest thing you've ever done in a video:** I almost flipped while strapped to the roof of a convertible during a trick shot video.
7	**If you weren't in Dude Perfect, you'd be:** A NASCAR driver or a horse jockey.
8	**One trick or shot you'd like to do:** A shot where Tyler would launch a donut hole off a skyscraper and land it directly in my mouth. Athlete!
9	**Favorite sport:** Basketball.
10	**When you're not making videos, you're . . . :** Pwning noobs* on the sticks in Xbox or ordering three separate meals from DoorDash. *Totally and utterly defeating new players.
11	**Life motto or personal tagline:** "If you ain't striving for birdies, what are you doing here?"

1	**One word to describe yourself:** Mysterious.
2	**An interesting fact about yourself:** I'm better at sports than climbing trees.
3	**Another interesting fact:** I was voted "most likable bear" in high school.
4	**Favorite video you've ever made:** Mascot School (look it up).
5	**Favorite trick you've done:** The trust shots are my favorite . . . unless they go wrong.
6	**Craziest thing you've ever done in a video:** Shooting a flaming basketball into a goal.
7	**If you weren't in Dude Perfect, you'd be:** A sideline sports reporter.
8	**One trick or shot you'd like to do:** The Dizzy Trust Shot—where I get dizzy and throw a ball and knock a cone off of Ty's head. (And hey, if I miss, I miss.)
9	**Favorite sport:** Log rolling.
10	**When you're not making videos, you're . . . :** Practicing stand-up comedy.
11	**Life motto or personal tagline:** "Keep your fur short and your dreams long."
12	**Bonus question: What's your real name? We won't tell anyone!** First name: Top Last name: Secret

DUDE PERFECT

NECESSITIES

Ready to have some fun? And make some shots and break some stuff? (Except for windows or bones!) Here are some of our basic necessities—the things we always have on hand for whatever crazy trick shot comes to mind. You never know when you might want to flip a water bottle or toss a Ping-Pong ball or make up a trick shot of your own!

YOU CAN GET STARTED WITH THESE BASICS:

- **BALLS:** Lots of them. Basketballs, baseballs, footballs, soccer balls, golf balls, Ping-Pong balls.

- **BASEBALL TEES:** For all things round.

- **BREAKAWAY BOTTLES:** They fit perfectly right over someone's head—especially twins! (See opposite page.)

- **WATER BOTTLES**

- **NERF DARTS:** You can never have enough of them.

- **NERF BLASTERS**

- **DUCT TAPE**

- **MASKING TAPE**

- **TARGETS:** We'll suggest these as we go.

- **PLASTIC OR DISPOSABLE CUPS, HOOPS, AND BUCKETS:** Yes, like an *actual* bucket.

"Sorry, dad, I can't wash your car today. I need this bucket for a book that I'm reading because I'm an incredible student."

—Suggested statement made by you. Deliver with confidence. Do not smile.

BREAKAWAY BOTTLES

FOR BEGINNERS

Although glass bottles are, in fact, breakable, the breakaway bottles we use are not made of glass at all. They're made of a special material that allows them to break easily and safely. These kinds of bottles are often called "sugar glass" because they are traditionally made of melted sugar for theater and movie special effects. However, our breakaway bottles are manufactured and not made of sugar. (We know this because we licked the first "sugar glass" bottle we bought, and it was a huge disappointment.)

CORY'S SUGAR GLASS BOTTLE FACTS:

- When broken over your head, the pain is level 1, the surprise is level 10, and the time it takes to get it out of your hair is level 8.

- The only ball that will not break a sugar glass bottle is a Ping-Pong ball.

- Smashing Ty over the head for my sneaky revenge break was a highlight of my life. Sometimes I still dream about it.

- As a target (arguably the best target out there), filling the bottle with colored powder increases the coolness (and unfortunately the cleanup time) significantly.

- If you accidentally leave one in the sun for too long, it can melt and fuse together, and actually become too hard. It will still break, but the pain reaches into level 6 range—not recommended.

- In "Restaurant Stereotypes," we used not only sugar glass bottles during the hilarious Rage Monster scene but also "breakaway" (essentially sugar glass) chairs.

COOL STUFF

There is nothing cooler than being able to *SAFELY* do trick shot after trick shot—all day—with no injuries or incidents to yourself or anyone around you. Part of what makes our team work so well is our commitment to everyone's safety. Even when it looks like we're being outrageous, we've put a lot of thought and preparation into our safety and the safety of our team. Think of it this way: Playing it safe will allow you to play longer and have the most fun while practicing shots and testing your personal limits.

HAVING A SUGAR GLASS BOTTLE
BROKEN OVER YOUR HEAD

1	Pain level
10	Surprise level
8	Cleanup level of getting it out of your hair

CORY'S BREAKAWAY BOTTLE RATINGS

HAVING A MELTED SUGAR GLASS BOTTLE
BROKEN OVER YOUR HEAD

5	Hardness level
6	Pain level
8	Regret level
100%	Not recommended!

ADDITIONAL SCOOP
ON BREAKAWAY BOTTLES

PING-PONG BALL:	The only ball that will not break a sugar glass bottle.
MOST BOTTLES BUSTED OVER SOMEONE'S HEAD:	Cory. Me. I never see it coming.
WORTH KNOWING:	Tape does not stick well to sugar glass bottles.
WORST-CASE SCENARIO:	Your trick shot attempt breaks only part of the bottle, but ALL the powder spills.
NED FORRESTER	Game show host known for breaking sugar glass bottles over his unsuspecting contestants' heads.

SUGAR GLASS RECIPE

Unlike the manufactured breakaway bottles we use, you can make real sugar glass for some epic, safe shattering. Use a cookie sheet for a windowpane shape. Or make your own drinking glass mold. Just be sure to use all metal, glass, or silicone dishes and utensils; the sugar liquid will be so hot it will melt plastic. (Sorry, Mom!)

WHAT YOU'LL NEED:

2 cups white sugar

$2/3$ cup corn syrup

$3/4$ cup water

Candy thermometer (optional)

Food coloring (optional)

Cookie sheet or silicone mold

Large pot

Cooking spray

INSTRUCTIONS:

1. Mix the sugar, corn syrup, and water in a large pot.

2. Heat the mixture on medium-low until it boils.

3. Boil for 10–15 minutes, until the mixture just begins to turn yellow. Or boil until a candy thermometer reaches 300 degrees.

4. If you don't have a candy thermometer, test for doneness by dropping a small spot of the sugar mixture into a bowl of ice water. If it hardens instantly, it's ready. If not, boil another minute and test again.

5. Remove the mixture from the stove. Mix in a few drops of food coloring if you want colored glass.

6. Spray a cookie sheet or silicone mold with cooking oil. Pour the liquid sugar onto the sheet or into the mold.

7. Cool for 2 hours, then remove from the cookie sheet or mold.

SUGAR "GLASSES" MOLD

TIP: Use heat-proof silicone cups to make breakaway glasses.

WHAT YOU'LL NEED:

An equal number of large and small silicone cups (*the small cups must be able to stack loosely inside the large cups*)

> Sugar glass recipe
>
> Cooking spray
>
> Rice, sugar, or dried beans (to weigh down the cups)

INSTRUCTIONS:

1. Do steps 1–5 of the sugar glass recipe.

2. Spray the inside of the large cups with cooking oil.

3. Fill each large cup with sugar liquid until it's about a third full.

4. Spray the outside of the small cups with oil and place each one inside a large cup.

5. Fill the small cups with something heavy—like rice, sugar, or dried beans.

6. Make sure the liquid sugar is about an inch below the tops of the cups. Pour more liquid in the large cups, if needed.

7. Cool for 2 hours, then gently remove your glasses.

DUDE PERFECT

HEADQUARTERS

THE DUDE PERFECT HEADQUARTERS is located in Frisco, Texas, which is part of the Dallas–Fort Worth metro area. Our first HQ was a 5,000-square-foot office. We loved it there (we were next door to an ice cream store) but quickly outgrew that space (thanks to fans like you) and knew we needed a bigger and better place to do all the absurd things we had in mind.

In 2016 we moved to a 35,000-square-foot space. That's *seven times* the room we had before and the size of seven and a half basketball courts! This space allows for offices, a kitchen, and a conference room, where—believe it or not—we actually, occasionally, sometimes, when we're forced to . . . do real work.

But let's get to the fun stuff!

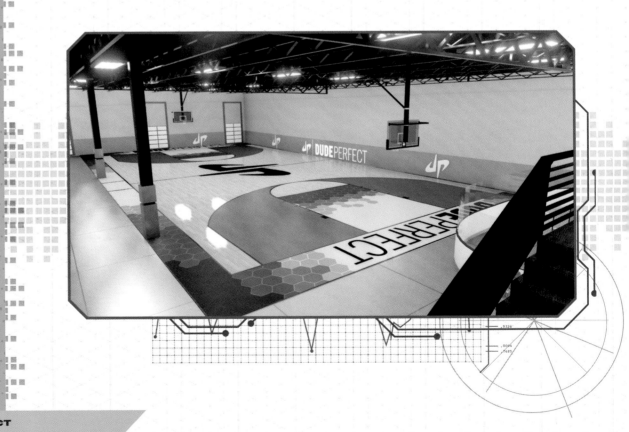

Inside HQ, we have a nine-hole golf course, a golf simulator, an NBA-sized basketball court, a hockey arena, a turf zone for football and soccer, tons of balls of every kind and all the sporting equipment to match, a media and gaming room with a giant projector, a car racetrack, lots of vehicles, an absurdly stocked pantry with candy and snacks, and enough open space for office-chair hockey, Wiffle ball, and whatever else we come up with.

Below are cool 3-D renderings of our space. To see the space in action, you should check out our video online called "DPHQ2 Trick Shots."

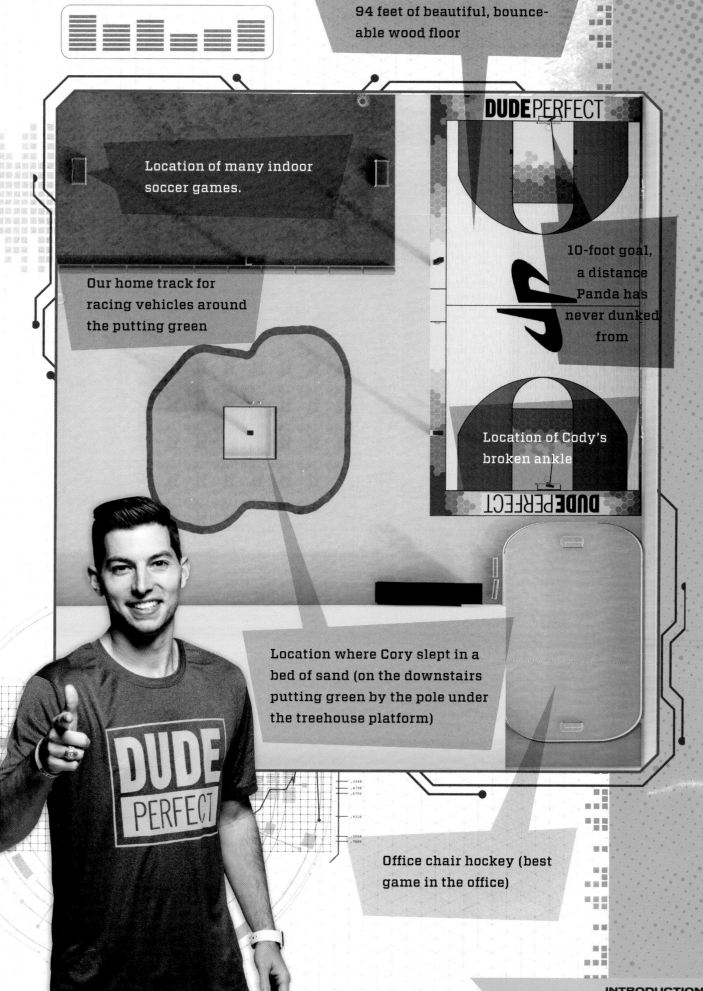

94 feet of beautiful, bounce-able wood floor

Location of many indoor soccer games.

Our home track for racing vehicles around the putting green

DUDEPERFECT

10-foot goal, a distance Panda has never dunked from

Location of Cody's broken ankle

Location where Cory slept in a bed of sand (on the downstairs putting green by the pole under the treehouse platform)

Office chair hockey (best game in the office)

· CHAPTER ONE ·

BASKETBALL

IT ALL BEGAN WITH A BACKYARD BASKETBALL SHOT. Tyler bet Garrett a sandwich that he could make a twenty-yard hook shot from the opposite side of the yard.

With a quiet *swish* and a loud "*Boom!*" Dude Perfect was born.

We've made a lot of crazy basketball shots over the years, but really, it all started when the five of us were simply having fun trying to make that very first shot. Then the competitive juices started flowing, so we pulled out a camera and started going bigger and bigger with each shot.

We get asked a lot of questions about basketball, so we wanted to include a little bit of DP insight here.

MOST DIFFICULT BASKETBALL SHOT TO MAKE

In 2012 we made the world's largest slingshot at Tyler's ranch in Texas with a cut-down tree and some duct tape. It took us two full days to build the slingshot and make that basket—the hardest trick shot we've made to this day! And don't worry, we planted a new tree!

EASIEST BASKETBALL SHOT TO MAKE

Every shot from our first video in the backyard! Haha! No, but really.

MISTY-EYED MEMORIES

Some of our favorite memories include late-night trick shot filming and Whataburger runs. And we'll never forget Ty making a basketball shot out of an airplane on the second try or trying to catch missed basketball shots from the top of sports stadiums—a brave but do-able achievement.

FUN FACT

What kind of sandwich had us put so much on the line? A giant club. Extra bacon.

SHOOTING WITH GIANT BASKETBALLS

Is it easier or more difficult shooting with giant basketballs? They are hard to throw for sure. But in general, since we are relatively closer to the hoop or target, we'd say it's easier.

WHAT'S HARDER—MAKING A BASKET FROM AN AIRPLANE OR A HELICOPTER?

We wouldn't want to try it again because we'd mess up our 50 percent shooting percentage. But currently we shoot better from airplanes!

"THIS SHOT DOESN'T EVEN HAVE A NAME. HOOHAH."

—TYLER

PRO TIP

THERE ARE FOUR KEYS TO THROWING A LONG BASKETBALL SHOT:

- Account for the wind. It matters.
- Throw the ball hard, up and out at a 45-degree angle. This will give you the most distance.
- Make adjustments if—and when—you miss.
- Try again. Be patient. It will be worth it.

A ball dropped from a high distance accelerates toward the ground. The force of gravity pulling the ball toward the Earth makes it speed up. This means the higher up you go, the faster the ball will drop. A ball thrown from a roof, for example, will be moving a lot more slowly as it nears the ground than one dropped from the top of a skyscraper (*like Ty's world-record height*).

If you do throw a ball from high enough (like a skyscraper), there are a few other forces to consider. The ball keeps accelerating from gravity. However, there is another force working against the ball called *wind resistance*. Wind resistance is basically friction in the air. Wind resistance can become so great that the ball will stop accelerating and reach a consistent speed—this is called *terminal velocity*.

If the ball is thrown from high enough with spin, there can also be something called the *Magnus Effect*. This means the spinning of the ball creates high and low pressure on different sides of the ball causing it to change course like a curveball! (Think of a Wiffle ball). For example, when Ty made his world-record shot from the sky-scraper, he had to consider the curve that the ball was going to have because of the spin he threw it with from the start.

TEN CLASSIC

DUDE PERFECT

BASKETBALL SHOTS

We've come a long way since Ty's very first *hoohah* in our original video. Since then, consistency and dreaming big has paid off. We've gone on to make some pretty epic shots if we do say so ourselves—some we never even dreamed of until we kept stretching our limits. It's hard to pick our favorites, but we've come up with a pretty solid list of Ten Classic Dude Perfect Basketball Shots for you to check out and maybe try for yourself.

TRICK SHOT 1

NO-LOOKER

As seen in our very first video, Ty sat in a chair and shot the ball backward. To make this shot, use one hand or both—just make sure you never look back. Your face should say, "This is going in. I do this all day long."

FULL COURT SHOT

This requires strength. And accuracy. And more strength. Get a running start. Think of it as a throw even more than a shot. By the way, this is expert-level stuff.

COOL STUFF

Don't be discouraged if you can't do all the long shots yet. As you get stronger, your distance will increase! *NEVER GIVE UP.*

TRICK SHOT 3

BEHIND THE BACKBOARD

First things first: before you get the ball through the net, you gotta get it *over* the backboard.

LASER SHOT

This one is all about speed, force, and precision. Launch the ball as hard and as far away as you can. Use the backboard for this one. That way, if you miss the swish a little high, you might get the bank to help you out.

FUN FACT

Did you know that Michael Jordan—arguably the greatest basketball player who ever lived—missed more than 9,000 shots in his career? But that never stopped him. He's known for saying, "The key to success is failure." And as we all know, practice makes perfect.

TRICK SHOT 5

BOUNCE OFF THINGS

We've used walls, rooftops, chimneys, vehicles, and everything else we can imagine to bounce balls into a basket. Don't have a basketball hoop nearby? Use portable items like trash bins, Hula-Hoops, or anything else as a target.

TRICK SHOT 6

ABOVE AND BEYOND

Make a shot *over* a wall. Or a fence. Or a house. Or a castle. Or a football stadium. Okay, maybe not *all* of those. But start small and keep going bigger and bigger and bigger. It's all about stretching your limits.

MOVING RIM

Yes, a moving target is harder. That's why it's cool. Our go-to is strapping the basketball goal into the back of a pickup truck.

COOL STUFF

We grew up watching some of the greatest basketball players—Michael Jordan, Luka Dončić, Dirk Nowitzki, LeBron James, Stephen Curry, and Kevin Durant—make incredible shots, over and over. We weren't headed toward the NBA, but players like these (and so many others) definitely inspired us to test our limits and get creative.

ON THE RUN

If the previous shot was a moving target, this one involves a moving shooter. It's the classic run and shoot. Or ride a skateboard and shoot. Or shoot from a bicycle or on skates. And yes, a small plane. It's anytime *you* are moving and the basket stays in place.

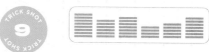

FROM GREAT HEIGHTS

Find the tallest height safely available. Then shoot from it. You might not be able to try from a professional stadium or over 500 feet up like we did for the Reunion Tower Shot, but it's fun making it from a balcony. Just remember to have an adult help you and be aware of everything below you.

JUMP, SKIP, HOP, FLIP

Try shooting while jumping or flipping off a trampoline or diving board. Whichever way you do it, adding some bouncy or flippy spice to your shot is always an attention-grabbing head turner.

· CHAPTER TWO ·

BLITZBALL

BLITZBALL: The amazing Wiffle ball with twice the curves and twice the distance—which means twice the fun!

The first time we saw that oddly shaped Wiffle ball, we knew we'd be great friends. Because of the many flat edges, this special ball curves *way* more than normal. Throw it with a lot of spin (snap your wrist), and you'll strike out your friends (or hit your target) all day long. Here are some of the things we get asked regarding Blitzball.

WHAT IS A TIP FOR HITTING A BLITZBALL?

Prayer. Lots of prayer.

DOES IT HURT TO BE HIT WITH A BLITZBALL?

It can. It depends who's throwing. Ty can throw some serious heat. It hurts more though to get struck out with one—not to mention your pride. And Ty did get hit in the face in "Blitzball Trick Shots." *OUCH.*

WHAT IS YOUR MOST DIFFICULT BLITZBALL TRICK SHOT?

Easy answer: the Hard Shot. At the beginning of "Blitzball Trick Shots 3," Ty throws a Blitzball through the windows of two crisscrossing trucks and hits a strike zone on the other side!

Life . . .
You're gonna get up
You're gonna get down
It's all about how you recover.
How do you rebound?
How do you bounce back?
Don't be a hacky sack!
Be a bouncy ball
Bounce right over that wall!

—A POEM BY TYLER TONEY,
INSPIRED BY BLITZBALL

BLITZBALL

GAMES AND CHALLENGES

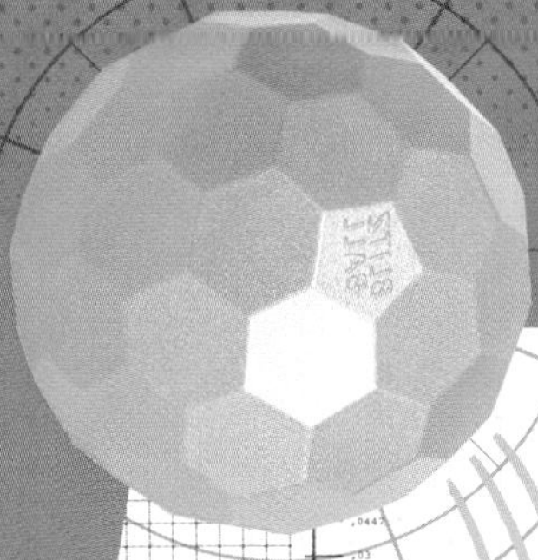

The Blitzball makes you feel like a Major League Baseball player. And a magician. But don't be over-confident, because you still never know where your throw might go!

You can play regular Blitzball pretty much anywhere as long as you have enough room. Baseball or softball fields are a great place to try out our first two challenges.

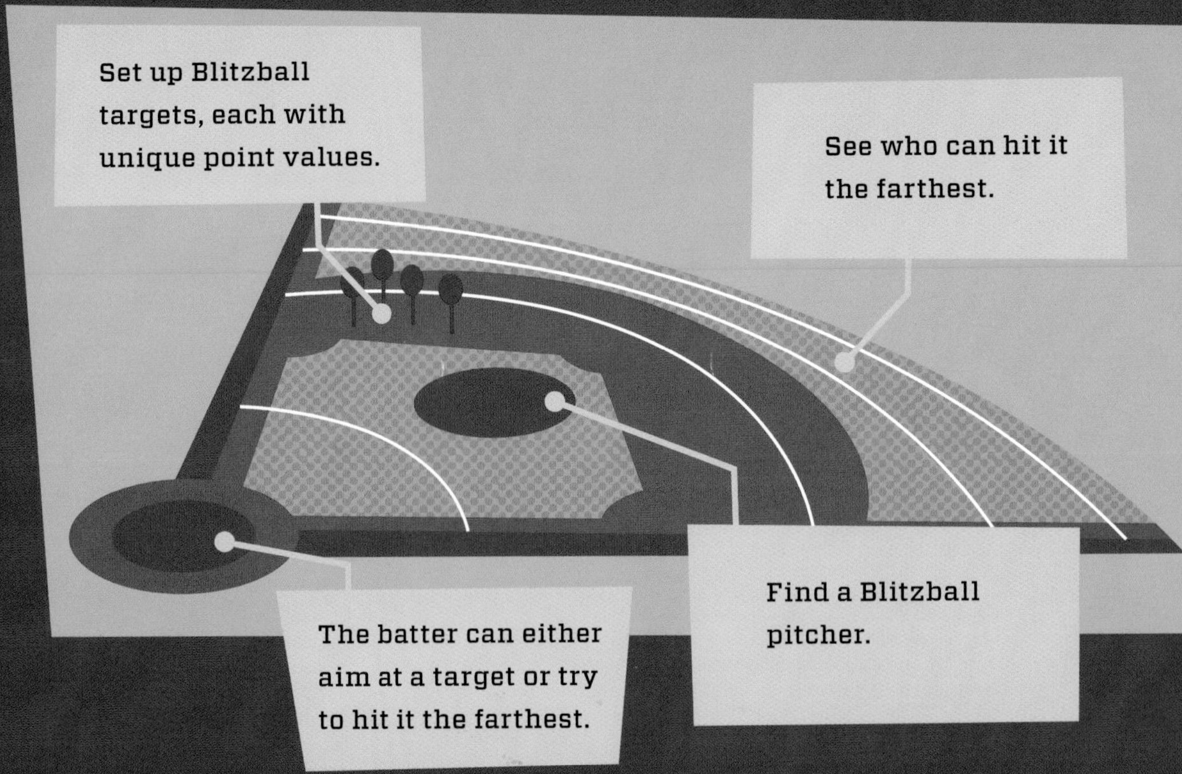

Set up Blitzball targets, each with unique point values.

See who can hit it the farthest.

The batter can either aim at a target or try to hit it the farthest.

Find a Blitzball pitcher.

HOW FAR CAN YOU HIT IT?

WHAT YOU'LL NEED:

- BLITZBALL
- BAT
- MEASURING TAPE

GET STARTED

STEP 1

Select a pitcher and a hitter.

STEP 2

The pitcher throws an easy pitch so the batter can hit it.

STEP 3

Repeat with another hitter. The longest distance wins.

STEP 4

Measure how far the ball goes.

BLAST A TARGET

GET STARTED

WHAT YOU'LL NEED:

- BLITZBALL
- TARGETS (*milk jug, breakable bottles, or other items that you can hit without being grounded for a month*)

STEP 1

Set up your targets.

STEP 2

Throw at your targets.

STEP 3

Hit your targets.

STEP 4

Clean up the mess you make.

MAKE IT THROUGH A RING

WHAT YOU'LL NEED:

- BLITZBALL
- ANY TYPE OF WIDE RING
- STRING OR TAPE TO HANG THE RING

GET STARTED

STEP 1

Hang the ring from a tree limb, deck, or something else in the air, or attach it to something like a post or tripod.

STEP 2

Get the ball through the hole.

BONUS

Set up a ring on top of a remote-controlled car, then make the shot while someone drives the car.

"LET'S GOOOO!"

STRIKE THE BALL THROUGH A TUNNEL

WHAT YOU'LL NEED:

- BLITZBALL
- A PIECE OF LARGE PLASTIC PIPE OR CARDBOARD TUBING

GET STARTED

STEP 1

Set up the tube or pipe so you can get the ball through it.

STEP 2

Throw the ball. Or if you're ambitious, use a bat to hit it and make it through the tube.

HOW TO MAKE A STICKY TARGET

1. Make your own sticky target at home. It's easy!

2. Get a rat trap—it's really sticky!

3. Tape the rat trap onto any surface: the wall, a Frisbee, a remote-controlled vehicle, pretty much anything. (Bonus points if the target moves.)

4. Throw or hit the Blitzball to not only strike the target but get it to stick!

PRO TIP: Do not—we repeat, do not—high-five the sticky target.

A regular Wiffle ball curves because of the spin from the thrower's hand. Imagine a pitcher throwing a curveball. They try to put "topspin" on the ball, making it spin forward. Topspin creates high pressure on the top of the ball and low pressure on the bottom of the ball. The difference in pressure on the top and bottom of the ball causes the ball to take an unexpected path or curve!

Imagine someone shakes up a bottle of soda. This produces really high pressure inside the bottle. When you open up the cap, all the air rushes out (along with the fizz). This is the air flowing from a *high* pressure to a *low* pressure. The same is true for a spinning ball! The air moves from high to low causing the ball to curve generally downward.

For a Wiffle ball, all of its holes allow air inside that whirls around and creates a pressure difference. This large difference in air pressure causes it to curve much more than a regular baseball or softball.

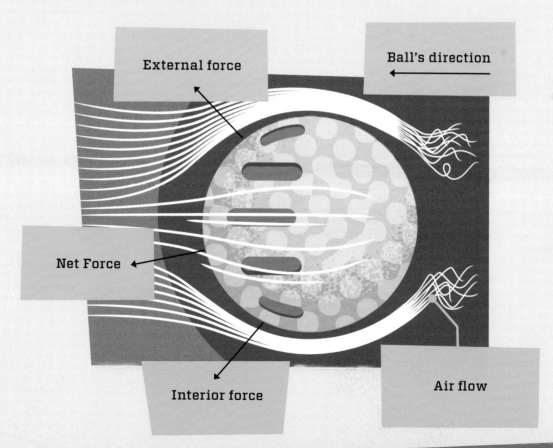

External force

Ball's direction

Net Force

Interior force

Air flow

· CHAPTER THREE ·

AIRPLANES

HERE'S THE REAL SCOOP on making the best loop de loops! DP is bringing you foam-filled fun like you've never seen. Aim, launch, and watch gravity and motion do their thing.

The first time we threw a large foam glider, we knew we'd found a *great* video idea. It is so incredibly satisfying to throw a smooth-sailing beauty all the way across a large room when the plane is in glider mode. Then when the plane is in gyrant mode, you introduce curves and flips and you're having a good time! (See more about glider modes on page 51.)

MEMORABLE SHOTS

The fun thing about these giant foam gliders is all the variety of curves, loops, and flight paths that can be done. Below are a handful of some of our favorite airplane shots so far.

TRIPLE HOOP LOOP DE LOOP

Through the bottom hoop. Looks good. Through the top hoop. Feels good. Back through the bottom hoop. It's all good!

LIMBO LANDER

Sneak underneath a beam, fly over another beam, then glide under another beam and land it.

MORE *MEMORABLE* SHOTS

FUN FACT

The Trip Flip, in "Airplane Trick Shots 2," took the longest out of any airplane shot we've attempted. This was the finale shot where the plane flips three times in a row before popping a balloon. We joke that it is the $9,000 shot because we rented out an arena for the day for $9,000. We had hopes of making lots of different shots, but this particular stunt ended up taking the entire day! And even better, we finally got it on what we had all decided was going to be the very last attempt of the day!

BLIND BALLOON BUSTER

A balloon plus a sharp, pointy device on the front of the plane is a recipe for BOOM!

NO-LOOKING LOOPER

Dart on glider + balloon on head = a trust
shot by Coby. He survived.

BARRELL ROLL BOMBER

We modified our plane's wings and sent it bursting through a balloon.
(Because everything's cooler when it bursts through a balloon.)

AND EVEN MORE
MEMORABLE SHOTS

AIRPLANE BOOMERANG

Hold a balloon with one hand. Throw a plane in a loop with the other. Make sure the plane bursts the balloon and not your head when it boomerangs back around!

DOUBLE BOTTLE BUST'N LASER SHOT
AIRPLANE TRICK SHOTS

DOUBLE BOTTLE BUST'N LASER SHOT

The signature shot from the first video, this stunt took a *lot* of tries because oftentimes one wing would hit one bottle and not the other. See how to set up the shot on page 50.

A toy glider is designed like a wing from an airplane. The same principles that help a plane fly allow a toy glider to fly as well. It all has to do with the shape of the wings.

The fast-moving air on top creates a lower-pressure area above the wing.

Wind moves faster over the curve on top of the wing than it moves over the flat surface on the bottom of the wing.

Air wants to move from high pressure to low pressure, so the air below the wing pushes up to try to get to the low-pressure area. This air movement creates lift that keeps the plane in the sky.

THIS CONCLUDES OUR
MEMORABLE SHOTS

BANKING GONGER

Everything is more fun when you have a gong. Set up a gong. Throw the glider. Account for wind. Wait for the gong.

TWIN SPIN

The twins never miss a chance to do a stunt together!

See how to set up this shot on page 52.

INTERNATIONAL SWISHER

When you need something delivered to you fast, call the Dude Perfect Express International Swisher. Standing from the balcony at DPHQ, Ty landed an International Swisher across the building into a basketball net. *SWISH!*

GLIDERS

GAMES AND CHALLENGES

THE DOUBLE BOTTLE BUST'N LASER SHOT

You can basically refer to us as rocket scientists because we have had another breakthrough in technology! Using No. 2 pencils, we're ready to bust some bottles.

WHAT YOU'LL NEED:

- LARGE FOAM PLANE (17- TO 22-INCH WINGS)
- SIX NO. 2 PENCILS. *Not No. 1 or No. 3 pencils. The secret ingredient is No. 2. Dos, amigos.*
- ELECTRICAL OR DUCT TAPE
- TWO BREAKABLE BOTTLES (*If you don't have sugar glass bottles, plastic bottles work great! It'll just be a little less breaking and more knocking over.*)
- TABLE, BOX, OR ANY FLAT SURFACE THAT WILL HOLD THE BOTTLES—*ideally three to four feet tall.*
- BROOM AND DUSTBIN

GET STARTED

STEP 1

Attach No. 2 pencils to the wings of your plane. Using strong electrical tape or duct tape, place three pencils end to end on the front of each wing.

STEP 2

Position your bottles fifteen inches apart on your table. Tape the bottoms of the bottles onto the table to help them stay in position.

PRO TIP

Always check your glider mode before throwing. Is your tail set on flip mode or glide mode? Seems simple, but there's nothing weirder than thinking you're about to send a plane to the other side of the room and instead it loops around and hits you in the back of the head. It's kind of like expecting to drink water and drinking Sprite instead. Sprite is great, but if you're expecting water, it'll really throw you off!

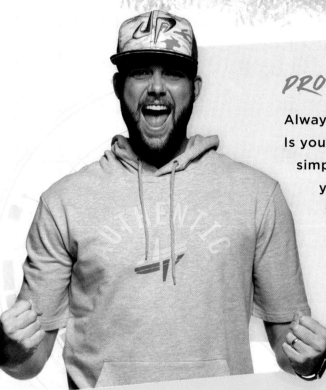

STEP 3

Stand thirty to forty feet from the bottles.

STEP 4

Throw. Hard. Raise the airplane slightly above your head depending on the height of the table and go for it.

STEP 5

Didn't make it on your first try? Make adjustments. (*This is key to succeeding with any trick, really.*) Move closer or farther away from the bottles. Throw it harder or softer, depending on where it lands.

STEP 6

SMASH the bottles!

STEP 7

Sweep up the bottles and clean up. (*Don't forget this part!*)

TRICK SHOT 16

THE TWIN SPIN

You don't have to have a twin to perform this shot. Just make sure you find a trusted friend who isn't going to throw a foam airplane into your face.

WHAT YOU'LL NEED:

- TWO PEOPLE (*Bonus points for twins.*)
- LIGHTWEIGHT FOAM AIRPLANES OF ANY SIZE. (*The larger, the better.*)
- SWEET SKILLS
- BLIND TRUST

GET STARTED

STEP 1

Grab your planes and stand twenty feet apart from each other, facing each other. Don't forget to adjust the mode!

STEP 2

Using both hands, hold the plane above your head. Aim straight and slightly to your right. (This helps to avoid mid-air collision.)

STEP 3

Gently launch the planes at the same time with enough velocity to make them loop twice. Make sure they don't touch each other as they turn up and over.

Once they make a full circle and begin to fall, try to catch the planes at the same time. You might have to run forward a bit.

STEP 5 The key is not to hit the other person's plane (or each other). *BONUS POINTS* if you both catch your plane!

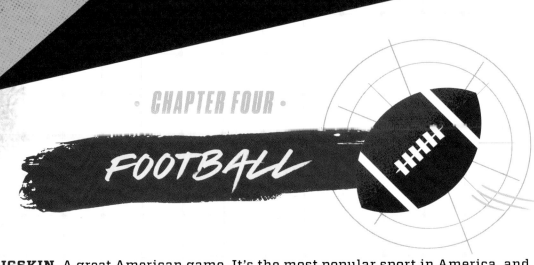

· CHAPTER FOUR ·

FOOTBALL

THE OL' PIGSKIN. A great American game. It's the most popular sport in America, and the second most popular sport is not even close. Football is known and loved, both in the sports world and in our videos.

We have done lots of tricks with footballs over the years. We've made far shots off of stadiums. We've caught one out of a helicopter. We've broken football world records, and unfortunately, also one of Cory's fingers during a blindfolded catch. (*He did break a world record in the process, so it's all good.*) Our point is simple: we love this funny-shaped ball.

Throwing a football for maximum speed and accuracy requires many things. First, a football throw is not just a movement of your arm. It is the movement of your whole body! It's all about transferring energy up through your body. This starts with your legs pushing against the ground to create a force. Then, your torso turns to transfer that energy and create more force. Finally, the whip of your arm, wrist, and hand transfer all the force you created into the ball. This long sequence of energy transfer and creation (and it's actually even more complicated than that) is what gives the ball all of its force and speed to travel far.

Raise football to ear level with laces facing away from you.

After releasing the ball, drop non-throwing arm to chest level.

Rotate torso for follow-through.

Start with feet shoulder-width apart.

Create a grounding force through your legs.

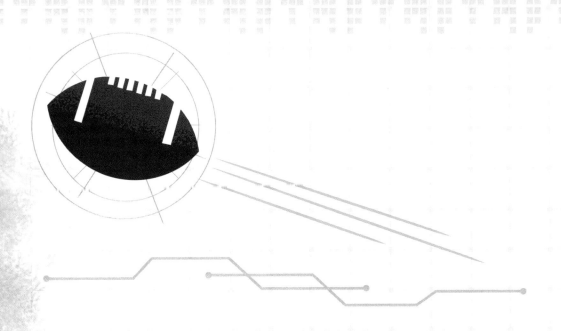

TIPS FOR THE PERFECT FOOTBALL THROW

To perfect your football throw, start by practicing each position below, one at a time.

Next, flow through each of the positions slowly until you can complete the entire throwing motion smoothly. (Don't worry about actually throwing and releasing the ball just yet.)

Last, practice throwing the ball at the end of the sequence gently, then gradually harder and harder.

Keep practicing. You can always get better! And trust us—you will.

FEET FIRST: Face sideways to your target with your throwing arm farthest from the target. Spread your feet as wide as your shoulders.

TRIANGLE: Hold the ball in front of you with your arms in a triangle. The ball is in front of your chest, and your elbows point down and away from your body. Be sure the last two or three fingers are on top of the ball's laces.

SHORT CIRCLE: Pull the ball back while swinging your elbow up until it's even with your hand. The ball stays at the same height in front of your chest.

L: Rotate your elbow to bring the ball up. Your arm is in an L-shape. The nose of the ball points away from the target.

ZERO: Swing your elbow forward and up to cock the ball back as your body twists toward the target and your weight shifts from your back foot to your front foot. Your elbow is slightly in front of your shoulder. This position is called "zero" because your shoulder is in a neutral position, without any strain on the joint. Your hand peels off the ball so that just your fingertips hold it.

ARM EXTENSION: Keeping your elbow in position, straighten your arm until the ball is over your head.

RELEASE: When your arm straightens, flick your wrist, push the ball with your fingertips, and release the ball. Your pointer finger should be the last part of your hand touching the ball in order to throw with a spiral.

FOLLOW THROUGH: Let your body continue the forward motion after you release the ball. Keep swinging your arm forward and step your back leg to meet your front leg.

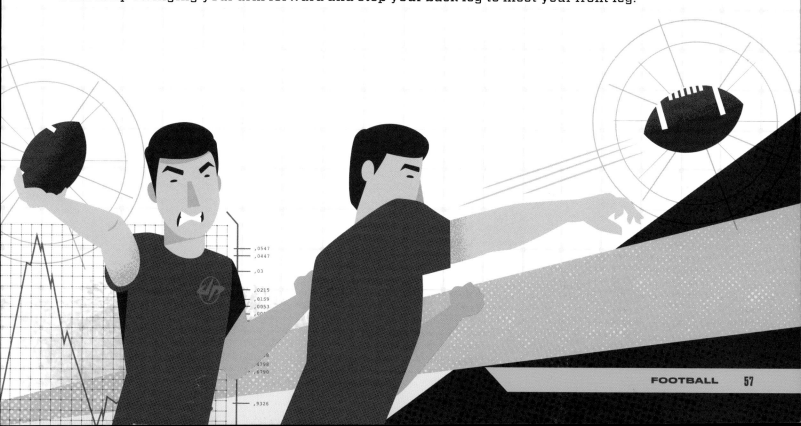

BASIC SHOTS

TRICK SHOT 17
THROUGH THE TIRE SWING

Throw a football and make it through a tire. To take this trick to the next level, try to make the shot while the tire spins around . . . and swings from left to right.

TRICK SHOT **18** TRICK SHOT

THE MOVING TARGET

Set up a target on the top of your parents' car or the back of their truck or on a golf cart—with the driver's permission! While they're driving, hit the target. Avoid hitting windows or people.

TRICK SHOT **19** TRICK SHOT

CLAY PIGEON SHOTS

Clay pigeon or clay target shooting has you shooting at flying objects commonly known as clay pigeons. You can use anything for this! Have someone toss up an item as high as they can and hit it with a football.

STADIUM SHOTS

PRO TIP

Ask a friend or family member to watch you and tell you when you need to make adjustments to your body. Or record yourself with video so you can see where you need to keep working.

TRICK SHOT 20

THE KNOCKDOWN RING RING RING RING SHOT

Set up four rings in a line facing the same direction. Spiral the football just right to make it through all of them. Bonus if you put a punch-out target at the end!

,0547
,0447
,03
,0215
,0159
,0053
,0000
,1454
,2350
,3348
,479
,679

THE SKINNY FIELD GOAL

You need to get out onto a football field for this (unless you have a field goal in your backyard). Place the ball on the sideline near the back of the end zone—just a few feet in front of the goal posts. Kick the ball just right so it curves and soars through the posts.

THE ROOFTOP SWISHER

Look—we know you're not throwing it from the roof of a stadium. But if your parents allow it (and we'll repeat again: *if your parents allow it*), throw a football from your roof or some high place, like a balcony. Set a basketball hoop below and make a basket.

INSANE

FOOTBALL

SKILLS BATTLE

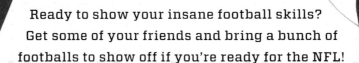

Ready to show your insane football skills?
Get some of your friends and bring a bunch of
footballs to show off if you're ready for the NFL!

WHAT YOU'LL NEED:

- FIVE OR MORE PLAYERS
- FOOTBALLS (*at least one per player*)
- ELECTRICAL TAPE
- TACKS
- BALLOONS (*four per player*)
- HEAVY BOOTS
- HELMETS (*optional*)
- COUCH

23 FOOTBALL SKILLS BATTLE

ROUND ONE: THROWING

GET STARTED

STEP 1 Find a wall that you can safely throw tacked footballs against.

STEP 2

Use electrical tape to attach a tack to the tip of a football.
BE CAREFUL! Have an adult help out with this.

A well-thrown football spirals through the air. A football with a perfect spiral can have a rotation of 400 to 600 RPM (revolutions per minute). The spin of the football does not allow the football to go farther, but it does allow the football's path to be more accurate and predictable. The best quarterbacks in the NFL throw a *great* spiral. This spiral reduces the amount of air resistance on the ball and allows the receiver and quarterback to be confident in the direction of the ball. A ball thrown without a spiral can still have just as much force and velocity, but without the spiral keeping it in a constant shape, it will be much harder for the receiver to know where the ball will go.

DID YOU KNOW?

,0547
,0447
,03
,0215
,0159
,0053
,0000
,1456
,2350
,3348
,4798
,6790
,9326
,0004
,7685

STEP 3

Blow up four balloons per player. Make the balloons four different sizes. Line up each player's balloons vertically on the wall. Put the biggest balloons at the top, with smaller balloons below. Note: Unless you have 452 footballs with tacks in them, you'll have to retrieve your footballs. Make sure while you do this someone doesn't hit you with their football.

STEP 4

Players line up. Someone says "Go!"

STEP 5 The first four players to pop all four balloons move on to round two.

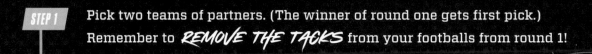

ROUND TWO: CATCHING

STEP 1 Pick two teams of partners. (The winner of round one gets first pick.) Remember to **REMOVE THE TACKS** from your footballs from round 1!

STEP 2 Choose a spot for the passers to throw from, ideally a high place like a playhouse or tree if you have one—or from very far away.

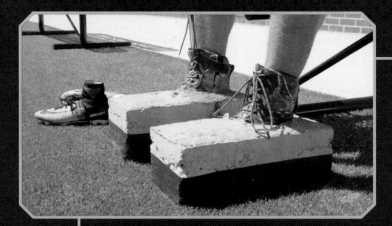

STEP 3 Make the boots difficult for the catcher to run in. (Ours were encased in concrete.) Tie the shoelaces together or attach weights to them. This makes the throw more important than the catch since the catcher can't move easily.

STEP 4 Each team throws the ball at the same time. The team that makes the first three catches goes to the final round.

FINAL ROUND: HUSTLE BALL

STEP 1

Find a couch. The two players sit on the couch with hands behind their backs.

STEP 2

Throw the ball at them.

STEP 3

The players then try to catch the ball or grab it from the other player. Wrestle them to the ground. Tackle them. Pull, push. Don't hit, bite, or poke.

STEP 4

Best of seven *WINS!*

FUN FACT

Hustle Ball is a game we invented in college. Basically, two guys sit on a couch and a football is thrown at them. The only rule is to get the ball. The only other rule is: *DO NOT HURT ANYONE.* The first to maintain possession wins. Just make sure there is nothing breakable nearby (unlike in the photo shown above).

.0547
.0447
.03
.0215
.0159
.0053
.0000
.1456
.2350
.3348
.4798
.6790
.9326
.0004
.7685

CHAPTER FIVE

PING-PONG

TABLE TENNIS WAS INVENTED IN AD 180 during the time of the Roman Empire. One night during a savage standoff while the Roman army was battling Germanic tribes, a German warrior tossed a hollow ball over to the Roman side. A Roman soldier happened to swat it with his small dagger that's called a pugio. The German soldier kept throwing the ball over, and the Roman kept hitting it back. They began to call it Pugio Ball, but after the Romans got rid of all the Germans, they decided to call it Ping-Pong based on the name of the German soldier, Sir Ping from the Pong Village.

Okay, fine. We just made up all of that after watching a movie. But wouldn't it be cool if that were true? Table tennis was invented in England as an indoor version of tennis. But this new style of tennis was created as a parlor game, originally played on dining room tables or pool tables. Players used any flat, hard surface as a paddle, anything from books to tops of cigar boxes. It went by several different names, including Whiff-Whaff. In 1901 J. Jaques & Son trademarked the name "Ping-Pong," which they later sold to Parker Brothers, who soon began enforcing the trademark. That's why the generic term *table tennis* has become the accepted name for the sport.

FUN FACT

There's a world record for almost everything, including for the "Most Ping-Pong balls held on the body in one minute." That record was achieved by Tony Flemming from the United Kingdom, on July 26, 2019. How many was Tony able to hold, you ask? A record-breaking 104 balls. How many can *you* hold? (P.S. Pockets don't count.)

HARDEST PING-PONG SHOTS

The chain reaction shots are by far the hardest because there are so many factors that could go wrong. We have spent multiple all-nighters trying to get one of these to work all the way through. But they're always worth it!

EASIEST PING-PONG SHOT

Technically the easiest shot to "make" was when we pranked Cory in "Ping-Pong Trick Shots 1" and told him he made three blind shots in a row. Definitely one of our best prank moments! Cory's best quote came after the second fake make: "Somebody put a ball in my hand!"

MOST SURPRISING SHOT

The chain reaction shots take the cake for sure, but after that, probably Cory's Ping-Pong trick shot in "Unpredictable Trick Shots" where he hid the "real" cup behind a printed piece of paper that was camouflaged with a photograph to look just like the table. Getting that to match was hard to do but looked super cool.

JUST A FEW HINTS TO HELP YOU SUCCEED:

- Tape a plastic card (like an old credit card) at the top of a can to use it as a backboard.

- Use soup cans, plastic cups, or Pringles cans for goals.

- Use any sort of hard, flat surface for bouncing off of: wood cutting board, piece of tile, baking sheet, frying pan, plate.

- When you're working on a tough shot, the key is less about technique and more about consistency—do it the same way every time until you get it!

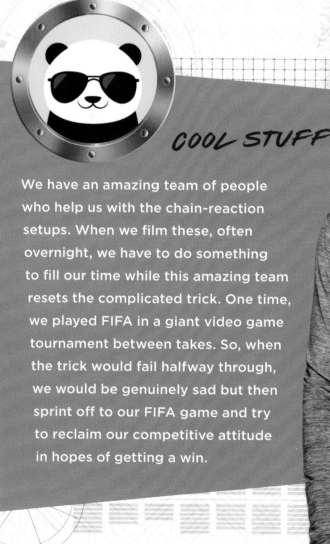

COOL STUFF

We have an amazing team of people who help us with the chain-reaction setups. When we film these, often overnight, we have to do something to fill our time while this amazing team resets the complicated trick. One time, we played FIFA in a giant video game tournament between takes. So, when the trick would fail halfway through, we would be genuinely sad but then sprint off to our FIFA game and try to reclaim our competitive attitude in hopes of getting a win.

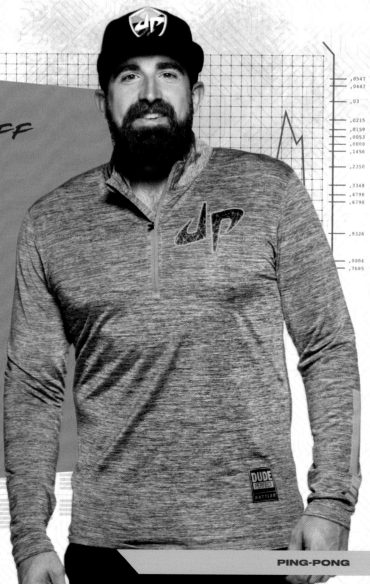

PING-PONG

TRICK SHOTS

24 THE FLYING CUP SHOT

Only try this shot from "Ping-Pong Trick Shots 3" if you are brave and patient. I'm serious, you've been warned. This is expert-level stuff. It took us about seven frustrating and exhilarating hours. But patience and determination definitely paid off.

THE FLYING CUP SHOT
PING PONG TRICK SHOTS 3

WHAT YOU'LL NEED:

- THREE OR MORE PEOPLE
- ONE 16-OUNCE PLASTIC CUP
- DUCT TAPE
- FRISBEE
- PING-PONG BALLS (*the more, the better*)

GET STARTED

STEP 1

Get three or more people together for the Flying Cup Shot. You'll need the flier, the receiver, and the shot taker.

STEP 2

Using heavy-duty duct tape, attach a 16-ounce plastic cup to the top and center of the Frisbee. This shall now and forever be known as the Official Flying Cup.

STEP 3

Get your stash of Ping-Pong balls ready and line up the flier and the receiver in a normal Frisbee-throwing range—about ten to fifteen feet apart to begin.

STEP 4

If you're the shot taker, stand somewhere in between, and just outside of the direct line of fire.

PRO TIP

It's always helpful to repeat things as consistently as possible. So, the Frisbee toss being accurate helps the Ping-Pong ball thrower be accurate and so on. Again, this is a hard shot, so ultimately it will take patience and reps, and the occasional refocus to get it done. Or as we say when we've lost focus after a lot of attempts, "Okay, I'm dialing back in."

,0547
,0447
,03
,0215
,0159
,0053
,0000
,1456
,2350
,3348
,4798
,6790
,9326
,0004
,7685

STEP 5

The flier sends the Flying Cup toward the receiver, and the shot taker aims the Ping-Pong ball to land in the Flying Cup mid-flight.

STEP 6

Did you make the shot? Sweet! *POUND IT, NOGGIN*—and quit while you're ahead. (Kidding! You're totally ready for the next shot now.) If you didn't make it this time, keep trying until you do. You've got this!

BONUS For a variation with more people, arrange the fliers and the receivers about ten to fifteen feet apart in a triangle if you're playing with four people, in a square if playing with five, and then in a circle with six or more. The shot taker stands in the middle and pivots or rotates as the shots are being taken around the triangle or square. Don't forget to take turns!

THE NO-LOOKER PRINGLES PYRAMID SHOT

Five thousand two hundred Pringles chips. That's how many we needed to eat before doing our No-Looker Pringles Pyramid Shot. Don't worry—it only took us a couple of days! We will do anything it takes to make sweet shots like this.

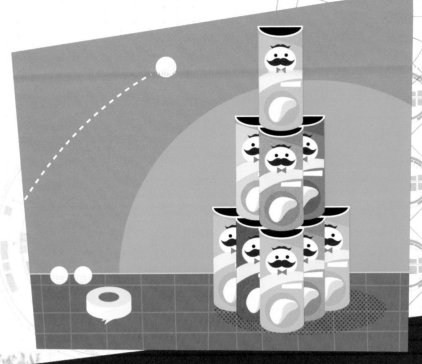

WHAT YOU'LL NEED:

- THREE TO FIFTY-FIVE EMPTY CANS
- GLUE OR TAPE
- PING-PONG BALLS

GET STARTED

PRO TIP

The Dudes used fifty-five cans: twenty on the bottom, sixteen on the next level up, twelve on the next, then six, then two, and then just one. Don't have fifty-five empty cans to spare? No worries. Even if you have only three cans (of any kind, really), make a simple pyramid on a table or counter. Unless you want to keep making the tower over and over, simply glue or tape the cans together for better stability. (Psst! Hey, even if you have only one can, you can still try this shot. Don't let that detail stop your No-Looker greatness!)

STEP 1

Make a tower of empty cans.

STEP 2 Stand about ten feet away, facing the tower, and shoot it until you make the shot into the top can.

One of the things that makes a Ping-Pong ball so unique compared to other balls is its weight. A Ping-Pong ball weighs only 2.7 grams (the weight of a penny). This allows you to do unique things with it. For example, you can suspend a Ping-Pong ball in mid-air using a hair dryer. The force exerted from the hair dryer is enough to hold this light ball up in the air. You can even move the ball with the force of your breath.

A Ping-Pong ball is able to curve greatly because of its light weight. A baseball curves because of high and low pressures on either side of the ball. Now imagine a spinning Ping-Pong ball creating these same high and low pressures. With the same force, the ball will have much more dramatic movement since it is so much lighter than a baseball or softball. If you put spin on a Ping-Pong ball with a paddle, you can see it spin through the air at a high speed!

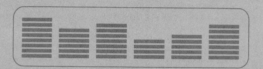

FUN FACT

Speaking of pyramids, there are more than 135 pyramids that have been discovered in Egypt, the most famous being the Great Pyramid of Giza. Its original height measured 481.4 feet—or 551 Pringles cans.

STEP 3

Whoa! You made it! Awesome. Now, turn around and throw it backward, over your head. (Not so easy without looking, eh? That's okay. Keep trying.)

STEP 4

Did you make it? *HIGH-FIVE!* Try it a little farther away to add more challenge— and don't forget to get a friend to record your greatness for ultimate bragging rights.

TRICK SHOT 26

THREE FOR THE SHOW

This trick is all about hand-eye coordination. Hand-eye coordination starts with you seeing something and processing it in your brain. This information then moves to your hands like lightning. Consider the information as lightning and the action as thunder. And when you make the shot ... *BOOM!* Electricity.

WHAT YOU'LL NEED:

- THREE PLASTIC CUPS
- THREE PING-PONG BALLS
- A TABLE OR A COUNTER

GET STARTED

STEP 1

Line up three plastic cups at the end of a counter or table, about three inches apart.

THREE FOR THE SHOW
PING PONG TRICK SHOTS 3

STEP 2

Wash one of the three balls and place it in your mouth. (Is washing necessary? No, but ew, you don't know where that thing's been ... or *do* you? And do not—we repeat—DO NOT swallow it. That's just weird.) Then hold the other two balls, one in each hand.

STEP 3

Exhale-launch the first ball out of your mouth so it bounces on the table and then lands in the middle cup.

STEP 4

Just after it bounces, toss the other two balls into the cups on the ends—ideally *without* letting them bounce.

STEP 5

Run around wild when you make this absurd shot!

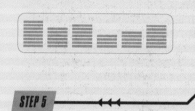

DID YOU KNOW?

Ping-Pong has come a long way from its days as a simple parlor game. In 1988 the game became an Olympic sport, with both singles and doubles competitions for men and women. The first two people to win the gold were Yoo Nam-kyu from South Korea and Chen Jing from China.

.0547
.0447

.03

.0215
.0159
.0053
.0000
.1456

.2350

.3348
.4798
.6790

.9326

.0004
.7685

6010

• CHAPTER SIX •

REMOTE CONTROL

TIME TO STOCK UP ON BATTERIES! Battles with remote-controlled cars can be endless. Race inside and outside using whatever sorts of fun items you can find to make a racetrack. Be creative and think outside the box. Or put them inside boxes! Create ridiculous courses and rambunctious crashes.

It's tough to beat a ridiculously fast RC car. Some of the ones we use top out at over 100 mph—yes, you read that correctly.

BUILDING AN EPIC JUMP

Assuming you're willing to risk some potential injury to your RC car, a big, epic jump is always a crowd favorite and a showstopper. The key to success is to make the transition onto the ramp smooth and the curve upward gradual enough so that the car doesn't "hit" halfway up the ramp.

And if you're not feeling particularly crafty, you can also buy a simple plastic ramp at a skateboarding store.

With an epic jump, you can create all kinds of trick shots of your own, but we'll get you started with a couple of our favorites.

PRO TIP

TIPS FOR MAKING THE PERFECT TRACK

- Use long surfaces like desks, couches, tables.

- Construct bridges out of cardboard boxes and other hard material. Or use duct tape for tricky bridges.

- Use boxes of all different levels to create ramps for the RC car to go up or down.

- Get different colors and different frequencies of cars so you can easily race others.

- Add lots of jumps and obstacles (banana peel corner is a DP fave).

- Create a jump and see who can go farthest.

INSANE
REMOTE CONTROL
TRICK SHOTS

TRICK SHOT 27

DART POPPER

Pointy objects and high-speed cars. What could go wrong?
We've provided a few options to make this one full of
dart-poppin' fun. Just . . . be careful, will ya?

GET STARTED

STEP 1

Tape a dart to the front of an RC car.

WHAT YOU'LL NEED:

- DART
- TAPE
- RC CAR
- BALLOONS

STEP 2

Blow up balloons
and scatter them
on the ground.

STEP 3

Pop the balloons!
*(AND DON'T POKE
ANYTHING ELSE
WITH THE DART.)*

BONUS!

Make this one into a game with
full-on bragging rights by getting a
friend and timing yourselves to see
who can pop the most in two minutes.

Remote-controlled cars use radio waves. That's why RC cars do not need cords between the remote and the car. The remote sends out a radio wave to the receiver located in the car. Each button or action on the remote sends a different signal to the receiver. The car's circuit board translates these different signals and tells the motor what to do. For example, a certain message might make the car go forward and another message will make the car go left.

Message receiver, which sends the message to the circuit board.

Remote control, which sends out a signal.

Circuit board, which translates the message and tells the motor what to do.

Remote Control Basics

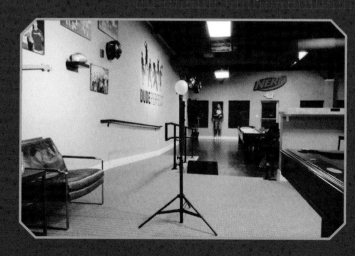

DOUBLE BONUS

Set up a ramp like we did, with an inflated balloon attached to the top of a stick or pole, and launch your dart-poppin' car off the ramp to burst the balloon.

TRICK SHOT 28

HIGH-SPEED PASS THROUGH

EXPERT ALERT! This one isn't for noobs. Race your car under a moving vehicle! We used a truck for ours, but we recommend trying this one with a friend on a bike—unless you have an adult willing to try this with their vehicle. Practice with a parked car or bike first.

As the bike or vehicle drives forward, steer your RC car straight at (and under) its wheels. Be sure to get permission from the rider or driver—and be careful to not become RC roadkill!

WHAT YOU'LL NEED:

- RC CAR
- TWO OR MORE PEOPLE
- A BICYCLE

GET STARTED

STEP 1
Have your friend ride their bike *SLOWLY* in a straight line in front of you so you can see and get a sense of the path. Then get your RC car ready and practice your path a few times *without* your friend riding their bike.

STEP 2

Once you feel confident, let 'er rip! Try to time it so the car goes under the bike frame, between the front and back tires. Here's the thing: there's no room for error in this trick. The average kids' bike frame is pretty small and depending on the size of your RC car . . . well . . . let's just say this isn't an easy one to practice. You either get it right on the first try or you don't, and you might end up with damage to your car. Remember to be *SAFE!*

STEP 3

Keep trying until you achieve total *VICTORY!*

STEP 4

Survey your RC car for damage. Ah, it's just a scratch. *WHAT'S NEXT?*

· CHAPTER SEVEN ·
NERF

NERF TOY PRODUCTS BEGAN IN 1969 when toy inventor Reynolds "Reyn" Winsor Guyer brought an idea for a foam ball to the game company Parker Brothers. A year later, the four-inch Nerf ball was released. They called it the "world's first official indoor ball."

Since then, Nerf has created an entire universe of fun: footballs, basketballs and rims, and of course, Nerf guns!

We've spent many hours having fun with Nerf toys.

"It's Nerf or nothin'!"

FAVORITE SHOTS MADE

We've made lots of fun, long throws into the basketball hoop with Nerf balls, but one of our favorites is Splashy Tennis Bucket when Coby made a full-court (across the whole tennis court) tennis bucket with our small Nerf basketball and basketball goal. A lesser known but personal favorite of ours is the Mini Pole, Mini Goal, Mini Ball Fish Swish where we fish a ball into a hoop with a small fishing pole (found halfway through "Giant Nerf Edition").

We're always trying to raise the bar with our trick shots. So, who knows what's in store for the future—maybe a trick shot on the moon?

Mini Pole, Mini Goal, Mini Ball Fish Swish
GIANT NERF EDITION

FUN FACT

Nerf inventor Reynolds "Reyn" Winsor Guyer also invented another popular toy that's still around today: Twister.

NERF SPORTS

TRICK SHOTS

Sometimes you don't need a set of Blasters and a hundred darts. Sometimes all you need is a football and basketball along with some imagination. With these, you can make trick shots pretty much anywhere.

The Nerf Vortex football is probably the easiest to throw because it flies and spirals beautifully straight every time! But if we could play with only one Nerf product, it'd be our Nerf Dude Perfect Bow and Arrow! The arrows fly sooo far. You have many choices of equipment when it comes to Nerf tricks.

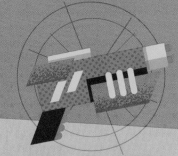

SUGGESTIONS FOR ITEMS TO USE:

- NERF FOAM BALL
- NERF BASKET
- NERF FOOTBALL
- NERF SPORTS VORTEX AERO HOWLER FOOTBALL
- PLASTIC TOSS RING
- TRAMPOLINE
- SWIMMING POOL

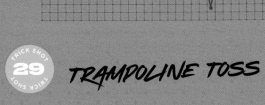

TRICK SHOT 29

TRAMPOLINE TOSS

Make a shot with a football (or another kind of ball) into a basketball hoop while jumping on the trampoline!

THE PLAYGROUND RAINBOW

TRICK SHOT 30

Throw a Nerf basketball over the swing set and playhouse. You don't have to see the target to hit it. Why not have someone *wear* the rim on their chest?

THE TOUCHDOWN

TRICK SHOT 31

Wanna feel like an NFL quarterback? Nerf Vortex footballs allow you to launch the ball as far as the NFL stars can! Fire off a missile and make it into a goal. Any goal.

THE DOUBLE WALL

Stuck indoors? Why not try to make some incredible shots using the walls? Bounce a mini basketball off a wall and get it through the hoop. Next, try to go for ricocheting off two walls. It helps if you can start from upstairs and have the rim positioned on the first floor (like in an entryway).

@DUDEPERFECT

@DUDEPERFECT

33 THE RINGER

Stand on the stairs and get ready. Have someone down below toss up a ring. The goal is to get the ball *through* the ring and then make the basket!

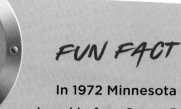

FUN FACT

In 1972 Minnesota Vikings All-Pro kicker Fred Cox, who played in four Super Bowls, invented the Nerf football. The idea came when a fan named John Mattox pitched Cox the idea for a game to help kids practice kicking footballs. Cox suggested the ball should be something light and made of foam to prevent kids from getting sore legs.

Cox and Mattox presented their idea to Parker Brothers, the toy manufacturer that released the Nerf ball. The company was only interested in the football, not the goal posts or the game concept. Soon after its release, the Nerf football became a sensation. Nine years later, the annual sales of the Nerf football reached eight million dollars!

34 THE FLIPPER

Trampoline shots are fun. You know what's even more fun? Making shots off a diving board. Position your hoop at the opposite end of the pool, then jump off the board and shoot. Bonus points for doing a flip!

@DUDEPERFECT

NERF BLASTERS

TRICK SHOTS

It's pretty straightforward. Just you, your Nerf Blaster, and hundreds of foam darts. Make shots behind your back or blindfolded. Hit moving targets. Create a series of targets. Ride something while firing. Set up chain reaction targets.

Are you ready to go? Arm yourself with as many darts as you can find and let's go have some fun!

WHAT YOU'LL DEFINITELY NEED:

- YOUR FAVORITE NERF BLASTER
- FOAM DARTS
- PATIENCE
- MORE FOAM DARTS
- EVEN MORE FOAM DARTS
- TARGETS

OPTIONAL NEEDS:

- SKATEBOARD OR SCOOTER
- GO-KART
- BALLOON
- BLINDFOLD
- BREAKABLE OR PLASTIC BOTTLES
- CUPS
- RINGERS
- LARGE ROLL OF TAPE

NO LOOK BALLOON POP

Make a shot while riding your skateboard or scooter. Oh, and you can't look. You have to make it behind your back.

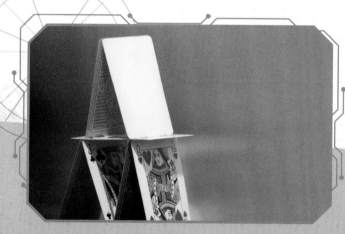

THE CARD PYRAMID

In our very first "Nerf Blasters Trick Shot" video, Cody confidently told us that he could set up a pyramid of cards (that we could then shoot at as a target). He used to do it "all the time" as a kid. It would be "no problem." He tried that day and could never do it without them falling. He gave up. We laughed. We still make fun of that bold statement. And to be clear, he has still never done it. But we have faith that you can do it. Set up a card pyramid of any size and shoot foam darts from across the room!

GLASS HALF-FULL OR HALF-EMPTY?

You make the call. Get somewhere high up off the ground and shoot a foam dart into a plastic cup filled halfway with water. See how far you can make it!

TRICK SHOT 38
THE BACK-TO-BACK NO-LOOKER

What's badder than popping a balloon behind your back? How about popping two? You'll need lots of balloons for this trick. We used helium-filled balloons, but you can use regular balloons too. Position two balloons, one above and one below. Remember this is a no-looker, so when you fire and pop the first, aim and hit your second balloon mark without turning around and looking.

PRO TIP Try this trick indoors so your balloons don't float away and litter. #DontMessWithTexasOrOtherPlaces

TRICK SHOT 39
THE VELCRO BULL'S-EYE

Do you have a dart board? If not, make your own with a piece of cardboard and markers. Now get some Velcro. Put one side of Velcro on the end of the dart, then put the other side in the center of the board. *FIRE!*

THE MINI SPINNY GONG SHOT

40

Get in a go-kart, on your bike, or onto anything that moves. The goal is to make a shot while riding. The smaller the target, the better. We love the gongs; they make a mini-clang when you shoot them, but metal pot lids or pie tins will work too.

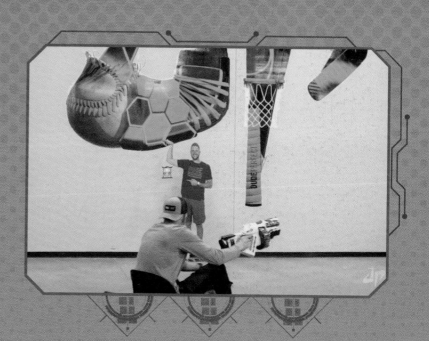

ELABORATE TARGETS

41

A pyramid of plastic cups. A set of tiny bowling pins. The number of targets you can aim and fire at is endless. Tape a plastic cup somewhere in the house and make the shot.

42

THE SPIN CYCLE

We love this one! And it's so easy to set up! Get a large roll of tape and hang it from the ceiling. Give it a good spin, and while it's spinning, fire a dart through the hole in the center of the tape!

NERF BOW

TRICK SHOTS

Look! Up in the sky! It's a bird! It's a plane! Wait . . . it's an arrow. Time to launch some foamy missiles at some unusual targets.

WHAT YOU'LL NEED:

- TOY BOW AND FOAM-TIPPED ARROWS OR FOAM DARTS
- ARCHERY OR FOAM TARGET
- BREAKABLE, SUGAR GLASS, OR PLASTIC BOTTLES
- EGGS
- HULA-HOOP
- TRICYCLE
- HELIUM BALLOON

COOL STUFF

We do a lot of crazy trick shots, but we also spend a lot of time planning and focusing on safety. This is one of the reasons we love soft, foam-based products. It's important that you use similar foam-based equipment when you try these trick shots. Stay cool and play it safe! #FoamForever

TRICK SHOT 43

MAX YOUR DISTANCE

See how far you can shoot your foam-tipped arrow or foam darts! Shoot, then put something on the ground to mark where it landed, and then try to beat that distance. *SUPER FUN!*

TRICK SHOT **44**

TRICYCLE BALLOON POPPER

Fill a large balloon with helium. If you're feeling adventurous, turn them into paint balloons! (See page 189 for how to make them.) Tie it to a tricycle or a bicycle. Get somebody brave to ride on the cycle, then aim your toy bow with foam-tipped arrow and . . . *BOOM!*

TRICK SHOT **45**

ROBIN HOOD ON THE MOVE

Set up a large target, such as a paper plate taped to a cone or a hoop hanging from a tree branch. While riding as a passenger in a go-kart, golf cart, or a car (with an adult's approval), shoot the foam-tipped arrow and make the bull's-eye!

FUN FACT

Cody and Ty often get looped into doing trust shots, which are shots where you have to trust the other person a lot to hit a target, which is usually on or near you. For one particular bow and arrow trust shot, Cody decided to up the stakes and make it a no-looker (Ty was displeased but trusting). Fortunately, his shot was accurate. Friendship maintained!

THE EGG SCRAMBLER

Take an egg—jumbo-sized recommended—and have a friend toss it into the air. Fire away with a toy bow and foam-tipped arrow! Bonus points for getting egg yolk on the thrower's head! Note: Do this one over a soft, grassy area since you might not make that first (or tenth) shot, and be careful to make sure no one else is around. *SAFETY FIRST!*

In archery, it's all about aerodynamics, the science of how objects move through air. For thousands of years, people have studied birds, arrows, and other flying things, but in the 1790s British scientist Sir George Cayley made a big step forward in aerodynamics. He identified the four forces of flight—weight, lift, drag, and thrust—and began to understand the relationships between them.

DID YOU KNOW?

PRO TIP

TIPS FOR SHOOTING A TOY BOW AND ARROW

1. Place your body sideways to your target.

2. Stand with your feet a little wider than your shoulders.

3. Pull the bow string back all the way.

4. When you draw the string back, your hand should be near your chin.

5. Aim at a 45-degree angle for maximum distance.

6. Start with large targets.

7. As you practice, make your targets smaller.

8. Accuracy is more important than power.

THE SWISHY SWISH

It's time for a mashup. Make a shot with a toy bow and foam-tipped arrow across the court into the basketball net.

CHAPTER EIGHT

WATER BOTTLES

WHEN WATER BOTTLE FLIPPING CAME ONTO THE SCENE, we knew this would be the perfect trick shot video for us. Most people have access to a water bottle, and that's really all it takes to have fun with this! Flipping a water bottle is oddly satisfying. We think that's a main reason people do it. It's hard but not too hard, and when you land it, you feel super cool. Trying to take that simple task and turning it into a series of videos with hundreds of millions of views? That's where a little extra creativity comes in.

Never has so much fun come from something as simple as a leftover water bottle. There's no cost spent, no electricity involved, no injuries to fear. It's just you and the bottle. One on one. Last person standing. Wait . . . make that last *bottle* standing.

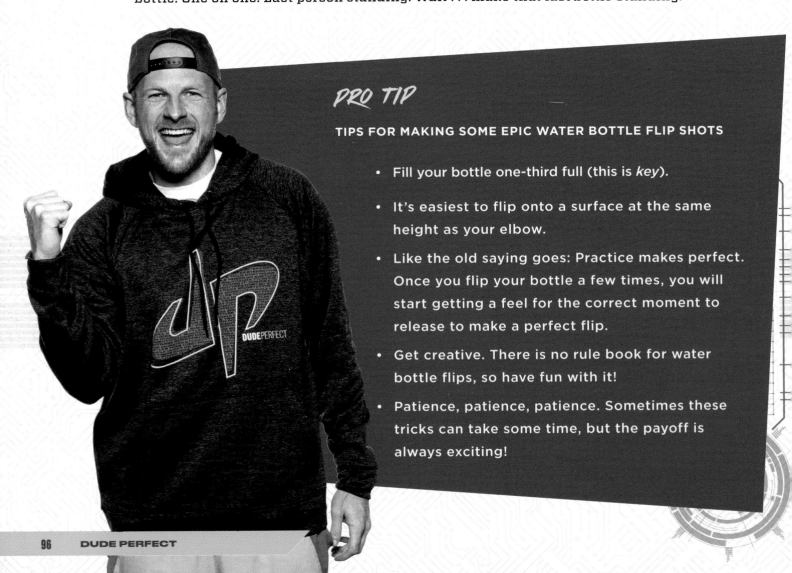

PRO TIP

TIPS FOR MAKING SOME EPIC WATER BOTTLE FLIP SHOTS

- Fill your bottle one-third full (this is *key*).

- It's easiest to flip onto a surface at the same height as your elbow.

- Like the old saying goes: Practice makes perfect. Once you flip your bottle a few times, you will start getting a feel for the correct moment to release to make a perfect flip.

- Get creative. There is no rule book for water bottle flips, so have fun with it!

- Patience, patience, patience. Sometimes these tricks can take some time, but the payoff is always exciting!

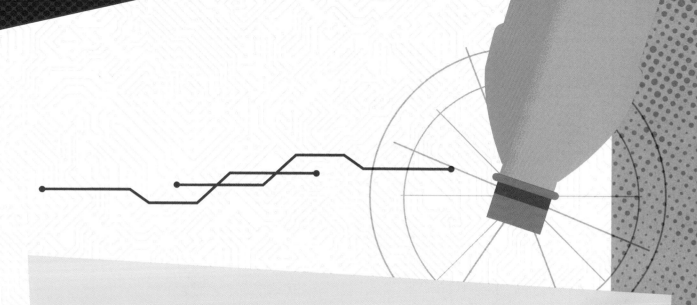

The secret to successfully flipping a water bottle comes down to one thing: *center of gravity*. An object's center of gravity is a point where the object's weight is even on all sides. For a regular-shaped solid object like a baseball, the center of gravity is the center of the object. But most objects have irregular shapes as well as heavier and lighter parts.

A plastic water bottle has very little weight, so its center of gravity is actually the center of gravity of the much heavier water *inside* the bottle. A bottle filled one-third with water has a much lower center of gravity than a full bottle. This becomes important when trying to land your flip. If a full bottle lands at a tilt, it will probably fall over because its center of gravity is farther from the bottle's base. However, if the bottle that is one-third full lands tilted, it is more likely to straighten out because its center of gravity is quite close to the bottle's base.

Try it for yourself! Fill one bottle full and fill a second bottle one-third full. Which is easier to land?

DID YOU KNOW?

HARDEST WATER BOTTLE SHOTS TO MAKE?

None of the shots we've made in our water bottle flip videos have been easy. Not only do you have to hit your intended target, but the bottle also has to flip and land correctly. Here are some of our most challenging tricks from our "Water Bottle Flip Editions 1-3," which you can find online.

GARRETT'S BIG BOTTLE TRUCK FLIP

"DON'T MESS WITH TEXAS."

"I FEEL KIND OF FLIPPY RIGHT NOW."

CORY'S 15 IN A ROW

15 IN A ROW
WATER BOTTLE FLIP EDITION

"SOMETIMES YOUR WATER'S JUST NOT COLD ENOUGH, SO YOU HAVE TO TOSS IT UP BY THE AIR-CONDITIONER."

COBY'S UP AND OVER

TY'S DOUBLE FLIP SLIDER

"NO WAY!"

"BAAAANG!"

COBY'S 4-BOTTLE FLIP

TY'S BEARD BALANCING BOTTLE FLIP

"HERE WE GO, BOYS!"

TY'S SUPER HIGH SKINNY RAIL FLIP

"TY'S HAD SOME CRAZY IDEAS, BUT THIS ONE MIGHT TOP THE LIST."

SUPER HIGH SKINNY RAIL FLIP
WATER BOTTLE FLIP EDITION

FUN FACT

Just like with all of our trick shots, it's super hard to pick our favorite. We only do shots that we really like and think that our fans will enjoy watching. If we have to choose, our current favorite is the new tablecloth pull from "Water Bottle Flip 3!" Which one is your favorite? Let us know!

CODY AND CORY'S TINY CUP BOTTLE FLIP

"TINY CUPS HAVE BIG IMPACT."

TY'S TABLECLOTH FLIP

When you bring water bottle flipping back for a third time, you have to do it in style.
And what's more stylish than a tablecloth-pulling flipper?

"WHAT DO WE DO TO FINISH OFF EVERY TRICK SHOT?"

"WE DO ANOTHER TRICK SHOT!"

BASIC WATER BOTTLE

FLIP SHOTS

The best thing about water bottle flip shots is that anybody can do them, and they can be done almost anywhere. Simply get an empty water bottle, fill it one-third full of water, then see how many places you can land it.

TRICK SHOT **48** TRICK SHOT

FUN ON A RAINY DAY

Stuck indoors? Here are just a few things you can flip your water bottles onto: tables, kitchen counters, top of the refrigerator, top edge of a door, on top or inside a washing machine or dryer, in your cubby, on stair steps, on the edge of the tub, on top of the entertainment center, on the arm of your couch, on your desk, on top of a book on your bookshelf . . .
Are you getting the picture?

49 TRICK SHOT

TWINS ROCK

Once you've mastered the water bottle flip, try flipping two at the same time. Make them land at the same time. On the same surface. Along the same ledge. It's twice as tricky and *DOUBLE THE FUN*.

50 TRICK SHOT

ADD A SLIDE

Find ways to make your water bottle slide before it flips. When attempting to make a water bottle slide, it's all about the sliding surface, the angle of the surface, and the level of your release. The surface should be as smooth as possible so that there is less friction created. Tables, wood or linoleum floor, and a railing all make great sliding surfaces. It also helps if the surface is flat or slopes down so that gravity helps pull the bottle. But the release is where the slide all comes together. Be sure to release the bottle as level as possible. If you toss it and it is leaning too much forward, back, or to a side, the bottle will probably end up falling. You won't get the smooth slide that you're aiming for.

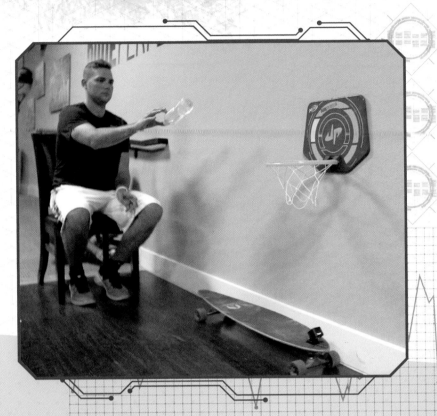

MOVING TARGETS

Try to land a water bottle on a skateboard, a remote-controlled car, or anything in motion. For the record, we don't recommend using a real car. Add a mini hoop and make it a *SWISHER!*

SKINNY RAILS

Everywhere you look, there are teeny, tiny rails and surfaces that a water bottle can land on. Get creative and start flipping away!

TRICK SHOT 53

FROM GREAT HEIGHTS

Flip a water bottle off stairs or a deck. Use gravity to your advantage.

TRICK SHOT 54

THE REVERSE CAP FLIP

Hold the bottle upside down and land it on its cap.

TRICK SHOT
55
TRICK SHOT

THE LADDER

Land six water bottles on a step ladder without any of them falling.

TRICK SHOT
56
TRICK SHOT

THE BIG JUG

Fill an empty giant water bottle or a two-liter bottle one-third full of water, then *FLIP*.

57

HOW MANY CAN YOU DO?

This one can be done anywhere. Simply see how many flips
you can do in a row. Can you beat Cory's fifteen?

FUN FACT

According to the Environmental Protection Agency, in 2018
27,030 tons of plastic made its way to U.S. landfills, compared
with a mere 390 tons in 1960. Water bottles make up a huge
portion of that. *REMEMBER TO RECYCLE!*

WATER BOTTLE

FLIP SHOTS

Here's where you have the opportunity to combine a water bottle with the wonderful wide world of sports! The options are endless. Use your imagination and create some awesome and memorable shots. Here are examples of some of our favorites.

TRICK SHOT 58 — THE BASEBALL SOCCER SMASHUP

WHAT YOU'LL NEED:

- BASEBALL BAT
- BASEBALL TEE
- SOCCER BALL
- HALF-FULL WATER BOTTLE
- SMALL TABLE OR PLATFORM

GET STARTED

STEP 1

Place a table next to the tee. Make sure the top of the table is a foot or two below the tee.

STEP 2

Place a soccer ball on the tee.

STEP 3   Set a water bottle on top of the soccer ball.

PRO TIP

Keep your eye on the ball. Try to hit the soccer ball directly in the middle, fast and hard, as if you were slicing it right through the middle. Also, use a half-full water bottle for this one.

STEP 4

Swing the bat and hit the soccer ball so that it lifts slightly up.

STEP 5

Watch that bottle turn once and land squarely on top of the table.

STEP 6

Did it work? If not, try again. Adjust how you hit the ball until you land it. *YOU'VE GOT THIS!*

FOOTBALL WATER BOTTLE FLIP SHOT

TRICK SHOT 59

WHAT YOU'LL NEED:

- FOOTBALL
- KICKING TEE
- WATER BOTTLE, ONE-THIRD FULL

GET STARTED

STEP 1

Place a football on a kicking tee.

STEP 2

Balance a water bottle on top of the football. This is the toughest part of the trick.

STEP 3

Make a silly announcement. "Now lining up for the game-winning kick in Super Bowl Three Thousand Seven Hundred and Sixty-two. One second left on the clock. The score is tied 27–27. A slight breeze coming in from the north."

STEP 4

Kick the ball—hard.

STEP 5

The football soars and the water bottle lands right-side up on the ground. *SCORE!*

GOLF WATER BOTTLE FLIP SHOT

WHAT YOU'LL NEED:

- WATER BOTTLE, ONE-THIRD FULL
- GOLF CLUB

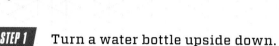

GET STARTED

STEP 1 Turn a water bottle upside down.

STEP 2

Grab a golf iron. Anything higher than a seven iron. Definitely don't use a five iron. Okay, just kidding—any iron will do.

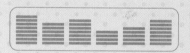

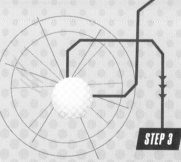

STEP 3

Hit it just right to make the water bottle flip one and a half times so it lands squarely on its bottom.

FRISBEE FLIP

61

WHAT YOU'LL NEED:

- FRISBEE
- HAT
- TAPE
- WATER BOTTLE, ONE-THIRD FULL
- MIRROR (optional)

GET STARTED

STEP 1

Tape the Frisbee to your head—wait, no, don't do that! Tape the Frisbee to a hat.

STEP 2

With the Frisbee securely balanced on your head, flip up the water bottle to land on the Frisbee.

PRO TIP

Perfect this trick in the mirror. Then impress your friends by landing it without looking!

STEP 3

Once you stick the landing, see how many times in a row you can do it!

62 THE DRIBBLE UP

WHAT YOU'LL NEED:

- WATER BOTTLE, ONE-THIRD FULL
- BASKETBALL
- 5-FOOT-TALL TABLE OR COUNTER

GET STARTED

STEP 1 Put a water bottle on a basketball.

STEP 2

Hold the basketball in your hands, then drop it.

STEP 3

Try to get the water bottle to flip up and over onto a five-foot-tall surface.

STEP 4

Victory dance optional.

TRICK SHOT 63 TRICK SHOT

TABLE TENNIS FLIP

GET STARTED

WHAT YOU'LL NEED:

- WATER BOTTLE, ONE-THIRD FULL
- PING-PONG PADDLE
- PING-PONG BALL
- TABLE

STEP 1 Hold a Ping-Pong paddle in one hand with a water bottle sitting on top of it.

STEP 2 Have a friend bounce a Ping-Pong ball toward you.

PRO TIP

Sometimes it's fun to mix up your flips by using colored water. Just a few drops of food coloring will do. (Fun Fact: It's also easier to see colored water on camera.)

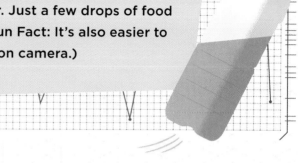

STEP 3 As the ball comes toward you, time your bottle flip so that you can flip the bottle and return the ball to the other side of the table. Hint: flip the bottle just as the ball bounces on the table.

STEP 4

After you've returned the ball to the other side of the table, be sure to catch your water bottle back on your paddle! This one takes some practice but is super cool once you've mastered it!

WATER BOTTLE

FLIP SHOTS

Now that you've mastered some of the basics, let's step it up a bit, shall we?

64 THE DOUBLE SLIP SLIDE

This one's fun! You'll want one large table and a smaller table about half as tall. The slippier the tables, the better! Wait, is *slippier* a word? Well, it is now!

WHAT YOU'LL NEED:

- WATER BOTTLE, ONE-THIRD FULL
- LIMBO STICK (a broom stick or tennis racket work well)
- LARGE TABLE
- SMALLER TABLE, ABOUT HALF AS TALL

GET STARTED

STEP 1

On the large table, set up a bar at about two-thirds the height of your water bottle. Make sure the bar doesn't move. We used a vise to hold down the bar, but you can use anything! Position a tennis racket between stacks of books or a broom between concrete blocks.

Set the short table a foot or two away from the big table.

Stand at the end of the big table.

Slide the water bottle across the tall table toward the bar fast enough so that the bottle flips over, does the limbo under the bar, and lands on the small table.

Make sure the bottle stops at the end of the small table. If it falls over, you gotta try again.

THE LONGBOARD TRIPLE FLIP

WHAT YOU'LL NEED:

- THREE WATER BOTTLES
- SKATEBOARD

STEP 1

Get your skateboard moving without you on it.

STEP 2

While walking behind it, flip over three water bottles in a row onto the skateboard.

PRO TIP

Skateboard + three water bottles = awesomeness. The key here is to get your board moving at just the right speed so that you can steadily walk behind it and flip over the bottles one at a time. Smooth. Steady. Sweet.

THE SWINGING SWINGSTALLER

STEP 1

Swing an empty swing.

WHAT YOU'LL NEED:

- SWING
- WATER BOTTLE, ONE-THIRD FULL

STEP 2

Flip a water bottle onto the moving swing.

"TELL ME THAT LANDED" SHOT

TRICK SHOT 67

WHAT YOU'LL NEED:

- WATER BOTTLE, ONE-THIRD FULL
- BASKETBALL BACKBOARD

STEP 1

For this no-looker, flip the water bottle over your head to land on the top edge of a basketball backboard—without looking.

STEP 2

Shout "Tell me that landed" before you even look!

PRO TIP

It should go without saying that when you flip water bottles, you should make sure the cap is screwed on. Well, during filming, Garrett didn't check the cap. When his flip didn't land, water spilled all over the table. And if you know Garrett—he hates a mess!

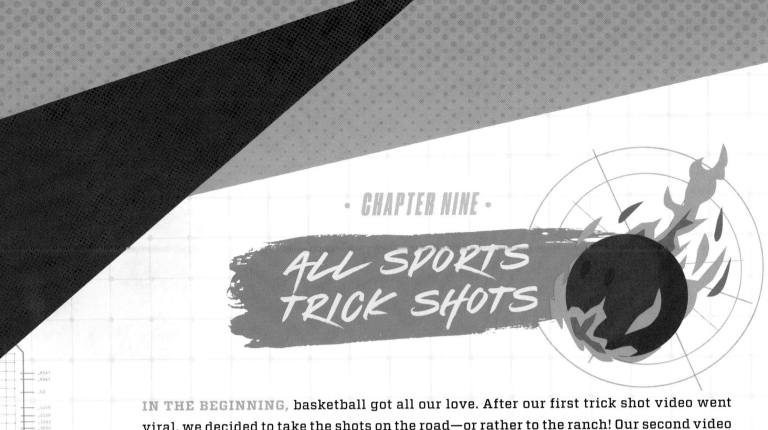

CHAPTER NINE

ALL SPORTS TRICK SHOTS

IN THE BEGINNING, basketball got all our love. After our first trick shot video went viral, we decided to take the shots on the road—or rather to the ranch! Our second video had shots on dirt roads and off tin roofs, dunks with tractors, and aimed from moving four-wheelers. But we quickly decided we needed to spread the love to other sports. (Making a golf shot with a basketball still uses a basketball, so that doesn't count.)

There were so many other sports we loved.

And there are some sports you might not even know about that do exist in other places in the world—not that we've tried any of these ourselves . . . yet. And if you've never heard of these before, we recommend checking them out online.

CHESS BOXING

Yes, this is a real sport. There are eleven rounds that alternate between six rounds of chess and five rounds of boxing. You can either knock your opponent out or get them in checkmate (but you can't knock them out *while* they're moving their chess piece).

FIREBALL SOCCER

We all love soccer. But we don't all love soccer when the soccer ball is replaced with a coconut . . . on fire. They do this in Indonesia. And supposedly southern parts of Texas.

EXTREME IRONING

Ironing is literally taken to a new level when someone is doing it on the edge of a mountain! For us, it's extreme when we actually decide to iron!

CHEESE ROLLING

Chase a gigantic cheese roll down an even more gigantic hill. The key is making it to the finish— or more importantly, *surviving*!

Okay, so when we decided to branch out to do videos with other sports, we decided not to go with any of these. (Cheese rolling, however, might be in our future!) We started with "Epic Football Trick Shots," taking the old pigskin places it's never been. Then came bow and arrow, volleyball, baseball, and on and on.

Pick a sport, and you can do all kinds of crazy and creative trick shots. Here are a few of our favorites you can try.

BASEBALL

TRICK SHOTS

Our parents always told us, "Don't play ball in the house." That's why we like to go outside to a baseball diamond, a sandlot, or a field. Hitting a softball or Wiffle ball is fun, but every now and then you need to hear that special crack of the bat against hard stitched cowhide.

WHAT YOU'LL NEED:

- AS MANY BASEBALLS AS YOU CAN GET
- TWO OR MORE PEOPLE, UNLESS YOU WANT TO WALK A LOT
- BASEBALL BAT AND MITT (we didn't need to tell you that)
- BASEBALL TEE
- TARGETS: GONG OR METAL POT LID, BUCKET OR BOWLING PINS
- BASEBALL OR FOOTBALL HELMET
- SCOOTER OR BIKE

EXTRA CREDIT:

- BASEBALL REBOUNDER
- MINI BASKETBALL GOAL

68 THE BAT SMASH GONGER

Baseball meet tee. Bat meet baseball. Baseball meet gong. This one is simple: set the ball on the tee and fire away. The key is to hit the target—any target—though the gong is the only one that clangs like that when you hit it. Or you can get a similar effect with a metal pot lid.

THE BOUNCE BACK SWISHER

Baseball rebounders are an excellent way to learn how to throw without needing to carry 457 balls with you. If you have one, position it so the baseball bounces up and over your head. You can have the ball end up in a bucket, or better yet, you can set up a mini basketball hoop to aim for.

THE BOUNCE BACK SWISHER
BASEBALL TRICK SHOTS

PRO TIP

A mini trampoline can be tilted on its side like a rebounder!

70 BUNT BUCKETS

Practicing bunts can be fun too! For this trick, you need a pitcher. First, set up a bucket of water a couple feet in front of you. To make a bunt, hold the bat straight up and allow the ball to contact it instead of swinging. The baseball will drop instead of fly. Try to get your bunt into the bucket of water.

71 THE BOWLING PIN STRIKE

Pitch the baseball and hit a bowling pin. If there's a way to set the pin above you, that's *EVEN BETTER.*

72 THROWING TO A BUDDY

Attach a mitt to the end of something that you ride, like a scooter or bicycle. Make sure the rider wears a baseball or football helmet. As the scooter or bike moves in a straight path, pitch the ball into the mitt without any help from the rider.

THROWING TO A BUDDY
BASEBALL TRICK SHOTS

PLUNGER

TRICK SHOTS

Forget about clogged toilets! Plungers are perfect for throwing.

WHAT YOU'LL NEED:

- PLUNGER (NEW!)
- LARGE TARGET: A HULA-HOOP, A PIECE OF PLYWOOD FOUR TO FIVE FEET TALL, OR A PLASTIC KIDDIE POOL

PRO TIP

TIPS FOR THROWING A PLUNGER

Pay attention! This is plunger-throwing gold you're about to read.

- First, hold the plunger at the bottom of the stick.

- Fully extend your arm in front of you.

- Bend only your forearm back toward you. Keep your arm still (don't go up or down). Do this a couple times to feel the movement.

- Stand about seven feet away from a flat, hard surface like a wall or door. Bend your forearm back, and then snap it forward, releasing the plunger at the last second.

- Notice the rotation and how the plunger hits the surface. Back up or scoot forward to correct. Throw with the same speed every time. When you get it to stick, you will have a huge smile on your face, maybe even the feeling that you've discovered a new superpower. It is just that satisfying.

- Theoretically, when you figure out the right distance away from the target for your personal throwing motion, you should be able to stick the plunger pretty consistently.

PRO TIP

We can't emphasize this enough: use a *clean* plunger!

THE SWINGING STICKER

Sit on a swing. Start swinging and throw the plunger toward a target.

THROUGH THE RING STICKER

Grab a plunger and a three-foot-wide Hula-Hoop. Have a friend toss the hoop in the air. As the hoop comes down, throw the plunger through the hoop, and stick it to a wall.

75

THE TRIP FLIP PLUNGE

Triple your personal plunging distance and go for the ultimate in plunging satisfaction. Stand three times the distance from your target. Throw hard and high to get maximum spins before the plunger sticks.

THE TRIP FLIP PLUNGE
PLUNGER TRICK SHOTS

FUN FACT

How was "Plunger Trick Shots" born? We had purchased a few plungers for props for some reason, and one day Tyler grabbed one while in the office. He turned to throw it at one of the doors and barely missed. He took a small step back, adjusted, and it stuck perfectly to the door! We all looked at each other and smiled. It was kind of magical . . . one of those funny *wow* moments that you just want to recreate. So that's exactly what we did . . . on camera. We canceled our plans for the next couple days and filmed "Plunger Trick Shots."

Did we break a lot of plungers? Maybe. Did we stick a few plunger handles through the drywall? Possibly. Was it a lot of fun? Definitely.

Making a plunger stick to a surface is all about air pressure. If you just place a plunger against the wall without pushing, the plunger falls right off. There is no suction. But if you push the plunger up against the wall (or throw it), suction keeps the plunger attached to the wall.

But what makes the suction? When the plunger is pushed or thrown, the rubber part of the plunger compresses (becomes smaller) and lets out air. This creates a lower pressure area inside the plunger bulb. That means the pressure outside the plunger is greater than the pressure inside. The higher pressure air from the outside presses on the plunger bulb while the lower pressure air inside the plunger *sucks* toward the wall: suction.

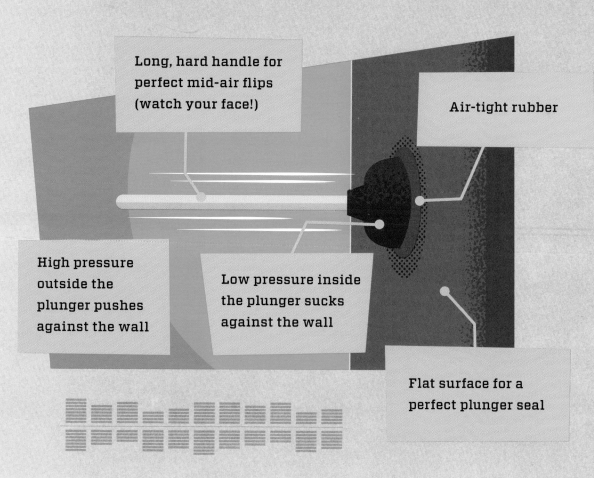

Long, hard handle for perfect mid-air flips (watch your face!)

Air-tight rubber

High pressure outside the plunger pushes against the wall

Low pressure inside the plunger sucks against the wall

Flat surface for a perfect plunger seal

CHAPTER TEN

REAL LIFE TRICK SHOTS

SOME OF OUR MOST POPULAR VIDEOS are our "Real Life Trick Shots" (RLTS). Maybe that's because everybody can do these! We started Dude Perfect on the idea of trick shots, so it's kind of funny that it took us so long to have a real life version!

Our first "Real Life Trick Shots" video was released on May 25, 2017. We had the idea for a while but wanted to make sure that we had enough shots to make the video really epic. We hoped that first video would be one of many more to come.

Trick shots don't always require a lot of time to set up. Life is full of opportunities for tossing, flipping, dropping, and flinging. Think of your house as the most elaborate jungle gym ever built. Inside, you have an endless number of items you can use like keys, clothes, hats, toothbrushes, towels, utensils, desk items, food, and of course, toilet paper rolls.

Most of the time, it's more important for a toss to be accurate than to be powerful. These shots have to land just right, so be aware of how hard you throw your items. Sometimes it actually helps to be gentle to nail the shot.

For example, when Coby was tossing the four pieces of bread into the toaster, he wasn't whipping the bread and throwing it right at the toaster. Instead, he was tossing the slices gently so that they wouldn't bounce or break. He was letting gravity do most of the work. (See page 140 for this trick shot.)

Our main piece of advice when attempting real life trick shots is to have fun. Really! These are some of the most exciting shots we've ever made, because the task you're trying to solve is so "normal" in everyday life. What's more fun than flipping a toothbrush right into the jar, or making your bed by throwing pillows backward over your head? Of course, always be careful. Sometimes the things that would seem to make the best trick shots aren't meant to be thrown or tossed, so be sure it isn't breakable and get permission from your parents before you end up breaking something valuable . . . or lighting the grass on fire.

FAVORITE REAL LIFE TRICK SHOTS

Real life trick shots are actually very challenging. When it comes to trick shots with basketballs, footballs, or other traditional sports equipment, we're used to the gear. We have been taught how to throw or kick the ball in a specific way, and we've been doing it for years. The movement is natural. But how many times have you practiced throwing a pair of keys or sliding a coaster? You feel like you are starting from the beginning and trying to teach yourself a skill that no one has mastered.

Here are some of our favorite shots we've made.

CORY: CLOSET HAT FLIP

This was a super fun sequence ending with the hat flip onto my head. Most of the time, the hat would rotate, and the hard bill would hit me directly in the face. So, when I finally got it so smoothly, I walked off with confidence like it was the very first try. (It wasn't.)

COBY: PAPER SHREDDER SHOT

Not to toot my own horn, but this is another *expert*-level shot. I'm not even convinced I could ever get another piece of paper into a shredder slot like this. Your margin of error is the thickness of a piece of paper!

CODY: DOUBLE TAKE KEY THROW

I spun because I was going to actually give up on this particular take because I didn't like how my approach was feeling. Then I just threw the keys toward the hook anyway. Nailed it! Turned out great.

TYLER: DPHQ SHOP FOUR-PART SHOT

Multiple-shot tricks are so hard because you have to hit them all in a row. For this shop cleanup shot, I swung a bucket onto a hook, threw a wound extension cord onto a hook, tossed a piece of wood over my head onto the wood rack, and then kicked a broom into a holder on the wall. Quick feet are the key here. When you miss a toss like this wood shot, you have to be able to get out of the way in a hurry (as you can see in the bloopers of this video).

GARRETT: GAME TOSS

I tossed the game disc right into the slot on the game console.
This is one of the highlights of my trick shot career. My surprised
expression says it all. It felt great, and the shot looked really cool!

FUN FACT

Between the first three Real Life
Trick Shot videos, there have been
over 150 shots made.

RLTS: BEHIND THE SCENES

Pssssst! We're gonna let you in on a little secret. Sure, we're proud of all the final, edited videos showing all of the epic and absurd real life trick shots we've made—some of them on the first try! But the real magic happens behind the scenes.

The good thing is that to make a RLTS, you don't need any special equipment or locations. There are endless opportunities! Look around your home for places to make some of these real life trick shots.

PLANNING

Whenever we get ready to film a trick shot video, we always start with a planning meeting where we talk through what we want the final result to look like and have each guy brainstorm some shots he wants to attempt. Sometimes it takes days, and sometimes it takes only thirty minutes. Once we have that meeting and everyone is sold on the concept, we then break out for filming.

FILMING

Rarely are we ever all in the same location when filming a Real Life Trick Shot video. We typically partner up with another Dude and also bring a video editor with us. That way, we can maximize our time and get as much filmed as possible. There aren't any slow-motion shots in RLTS, so we need to capture even more content to get a decently long video. Sometimes we nail our list of ideas, and other times we make up a number of different shots off the cuff. We typically plan for a full week of filming to capture all the content we need for one Real Life Trick Shot video.

SPILLING

We've learned over the years to expect the unexpected. When we were filming "Real Life Trick Shots 3," our first shot of the day was Ty throwing a container of cheeseballs over his shoulder, over a store shelving display, and into Cory's shopping cart. On Ty's first toss, he missed the shopping cart and the entire container of cheeseballs exploded and went everywhere! You don't realize how many come in one container until *every* cheeseball rushes out onto the tile floor. Each spill or mishap can add anywhere from fifteen minutes to an hour or more, depending on how much we messed up. It made for a funny blooper though!

TRICK SHOT 76

HOOK 'EM COWBOY

Let's start off with one of the most basic things that we use all the time: hooks! The average household in America holds 17.4 different types of hooks. Okay, we just made that up. But if you start counting, you'll be surprised just how many hooks there are in your home. This means you have countless options for tossing, flipping, and hooking thousands of items.

THE TOWEL RACK
Could have a hook. Could be a rail. Could be a ring. Maybe just a nail.

THE KEY RACK
Smaller than the coat rack but the same idea. Usually mounted on a wall.

PICTURE HANGER HOOKS
They're tiny but mighty.

MOP AND BROOM HOLDER
Can you hook the broom in its place?

EQUIPMENT RACK
The fun doesn't have to end when the game ends. Hook your helmets, bats, rackets, balls, and pads into place.

THE COAT RACK

Often found in a mudroom or hallway. Usually featuring multiple hooks. Sometimes even with designated names behind them. Of course, there is also the good ol' coat rack that looks like a skinny robot with multiple arms and horns sticking out of its head.

IN THE KITCHEN

WITH THE DUDES

We have something to confess. (*Hopefully our wives aren't reading this!*) A lot of the Real Life Trick Shot filming is done in our homes or at the Dude Perfect headquarters. Unfortunately, we've broken a number of items and have made quite a few messes.

Utensils and silverware, pots and pans, pancakes and Hot Pockets . . . the options for RLTS are endless. Take a look around the kitchen for all the trick shots you can do. (Let's hold off on the knives and cutlery though.)

TRICK SHOT 77

THE TOASTER

The more slots, the better. Toss two or four pieces of toast into the toaster, *using only one hand.* Or wing in some waffles.

TRICK SHOT 78

THE ISLAND

Perfect for sliding and experimenting. Launch a bottle of orange juice into the side door of your refrigerator. Flip a straw into a soda bottle. Toss the spatula into its holder. Hurl chocolate chip cookie dough onto a baking pan. (Actually, maybe *hurl* is the wrong word to use here.)

"CAKE ME"

Another word for love in our group is "Cake Me." Actually, that's two words. At the stove, flip a cooled-off pancake behind your back and make it land on someone's plate.

THREE SPOONS AND A DUDE

Flipping one spoon into a cup is cool but flipping three of them at the same time is epic! Place three cups or mugs side by side on a table, then place a spoon with the scoop part facing you in front of the mugs. Position three other spoons upside down with the scoop parts sitting on the end of the first spoon. Make a fist and gently tap the scoop of the first spoon to flip the other three into separate mugs. *POW!*

81 LET IT FLY

LET SOME NONBREAKABLE ITEMS FLY BACK TO THEIR HOME.

- Launch a wooden spoon back into its caddy.
- Send a roll of paper towels spinning and landing onto a holder.
- Chuck a cereal box sideways so it slips into the cabinet.
- Toss a coffee pod into a Keurig machine.

82 THE LAZY DISHWASHER LOADER

Putting utensils into a dishwasher can be so difficult. You know—bending over, picking out that specific spot, getting the fork tangled with the spoons. It just takes *so much work*. Why not just sit and fling a plastic spatula across the kitchen into the dishwasher?

83 DOIN' THE DISHES

Make your parents proud and offer to do the dishes! Plastic cups and bowls are perfect for lobbing and tossing! As for glass and ceramic . . . maybe just gently slide those into the dishwasher.

84 HOOK SHOT

Hook an orange.
Or an apple.
Or a banana.
Or a kiwi.

Attempt to make a basket with pretty much any fruit or vegetable into a blender (maybe skip the spinach). Smoothie, anyone? *POUND IT!*

85 FLIPPED OUT

There are *so many* things you can flip in a kitchen! Try a straw flip into a bottle or cup. Spice bottle flip behind the back into the spice rack. Fridge magnet flip back on the fridge door. A tea bag flip into a cup. A spatula flip into the drawer or basket.

86 OVEN MITT TOSS

Try tossing an oven mitt onto someone's hand.

CLEANING UP

WITH THE DUDES

Balls left on the driveway. Clothes on the floor. A backpack dropped in the middle of the family room. Why not have some fun while cleaning up? Here are some suggestions on how to tidy up while also challenging yourself!

87 THROW IT AWAY

Literally. Think of creative ways to throw your things into the waste bin. Whip them across the room. Whack them with a broom. Whirl them with a plume. Okay, sorry—we almost had a Dr. Seuss thing going there, but you get the idea.

88 GARBAGE BAG TOSS

Nobody likes to take out the trash. Attempting to make a basket with your garbage bag is a whole different matter! Make sure the bag is tied tight. Then look for ways to send it flying into the garbage can.

89 HANG IT UP

Hang a shirt on a hanger, then toss it onto the rack. Next try two shirts with each hand. How about three hangers in one hand?

EVERYTHING IN ITS RIGHT PLACE

Bounce basketballs back onto their rack or into a storage bin. Keep everything in a sports locker? Toss, flip, and shoot all your balls and gear into it. Lob that spare tennis ball back into its tube. Kick a soccer ball onto a rolling sports ball storage cart.

CLOSET CLEANUP WITH CODY

Smelly socks? Behind-the-back shot into the hamper. Shoes? Lob onto a shelf or rack. Hat? Fling onto a shelf.

BATHROOM BREAK

There are lots of shots you can make in the bathroom—toothbrush in cup, towel toss, toilet paper onto ringer.

· CHAPTER ELEVEN ·

BATTLES

THE THRILL OF VICTORY and the agony of defeat. Water slides plus Nerf guns. Trampolines with charades. Oversized *everything*.

Battles are awesome when you mix and match sports. Or when you simply have ten thousand pounds of bubble wrap! Hey, ten thousand of anything makes for an interesting situation.

We could probably do an entire book just on battles, but for now, here's a solid overview of our battle history, along with details on how to set up some of our most fun battles for yourself.

LIST OF BATTLES

Part of the fun of a battle is coming up with the structure. Most battles have several qualifying rounds. Sometimes the losers are eliminated, and sometimes the winners advance, but either way, an exciting finale leads to the crowning of an ultimate battle champion. You can either visit our Dude Perfect YouTube channel or search the internet for Dude Perfect with a particular battle name to see the battles in action!

BATTLE	WINNER
Paper Airplane Battle	CODY
Go-Kart Battle	PANDA
Bubble Wrap Battle	TYLER
Shark Fishing Battle	TYLER
Dizzy Sports Battle	TYLER
iPhone Game Battle	CORY
All Sports Golf Battle	GARRETT
Dizzy Sports Battle 2	TYLER
RC Battle	CODY
Nerf Blasters Battle	TYLER
Plastic Golf Club Battle	TYLER
Slip and Slide Football Battle	CODY
Bubble Gum Blowing Battle	TYLER
Snow Sports Battle	TYLER
Backyard Games Battle	TYLER
All Sports Bowling Battle	GARRETT

BATTLE	WINNER
Archery Kart Battle	CORY & COBY
Mountain Top Snow Battle	TYLER
Giant Basketball Arcade Battle	TYLER
Giant Pictionary Battle	TYLER & GARRETT
Lawnmower Racing Battle	GARRETT
Drone Racing Battle	TYLER
Endless Ducker Battle	CORY
Trampoline Charades Battle	GARRETT & CODY
Metal Detector Battle	CODY
Giant Warship Battle	GARRETT, TYLER, & PANDA
Drone Hunting Battle	TYLER & CORY TIED
Extreme Weather Golf Battle	CORY
Virtual Reality Battle	TYLER
Giant Sumo Battle	COBY
Stunt Driving Battle	GARRETT
Nerf Slip and Slide Battle	TYLER
Build a Boat Battle	CORY
Freeze Frame Football Battle	CODY

BATTLE	WINNER
Freeze Frame Football Battle	CODY
All Sports Golf Battle 2	TYLER
Model Rocket Battle	GARRETT
Deep Sea Fishing Battle	TYLER
Giant Darts Battle	GARRETT
Go-Kart Soccer	COBY, CORY, & TYLER
Dirt Bike Battle	TYLER
All Sports Golf Battle 3	GARRETT
Nerf Blasters Floating Island Battle	CODY
High Speed Sports Battle	TYLER
Airsoft Battle Royale	CODY
Model Rocket Battle 2	CORY
Nerf Fortnite Blasters Battle	CORY
All Sports Baseball Battle	CORY
Metal Detector Battle 2	CODY
RC Airplane Battle	COBY
Bass Fishing Battle	TYLER
Helicopter Battleship	TYLER (& A LITTLE BIT OF CODY)

JUST THE STATS

BOTTOM LINE: Who's the All Sports Battle champ? It's not even close: Ty is (so far) the Battle champ. This tells you all you need to know.

PLAYER	WINS	FINALE APPEARANCES
	21	41
	9	25
	10	20
	8	12
	3	20
	2	0

"FUN FACT, GUYS: COBY, YET AGAIN, CANNOT WIN A BATTLE!"

—CODY JONES

WHY DID IT TAKE SO LONG FOR COBY TO WIN A BATTLE?

It took Coby four long years to win a battle, but that wasn't due to a lack of effort! As the great football coach Vince Lombardi once said, "Winning is a habit. Unfortunately, so is losing." Kids would come up to him and ask, "Coby, are you ever going to win a battle?" And he knew he was in a bad place when he started responding with, "I don't know. I just don't know."

Coby did finally win his first battle in Giant Sumo Battle. He won his second battle in RC Airplane Battle. Also, Coby has tied with Garrett for the most finale appearances— twenty, at the time of writing this book.

Here's a little life lesson courtesy of Coby's heartbreak: If you think about it, everyone is fighting a battle of some kind and each person has his or her own levels of difficulty needed to overcome them. However, with perseverance, dedication, and hard work, you can win!

EACH DUDE'S FAVORITE BATTLE

AIRSOFT BATTLE ROYALE. I loved squaring off with the other guys in a sweet location, trying to pop their balloons before they pop mine. A simple idea, but a blast to play and a blast to watch!

TYLER

POP EACH OTHER'S BALLOONS AND BE THE LAST MAN STANDING

36.59553,-76.28676

ALL SPORTS GOLF BATTLE 3. We all love golf, but we figured golf would be even better without, well, the golf part. We play on a golf course and use all the sports *except* golf clubs. The rules are simple: Use each item once, then lose it. First to finish the hole (least strokes) is the winner!

GARRETT

COBY

GIANT SUMO BATTLE. (First Battle Win) This video will always hold a special place in my heart. I fought my heart out and was finally able to hoist that trophy with a smile on my face. The guys decided to throw me a parade to celebrate. In front of over a thousand people, I rode in dressed as a king on a horse (yes, actually). Fun fact: At the time, I had just started dating my now wife. She came to support me at my parade and so our first picture together was with me dressed as a king.

NERF FORTNITE BLASTERS BATTLE. I loved this battle—an obstacle course spread out with targets for us to shoot with our Nerf Blasters as we went! I was trying to win my third battle in a row, and when I did, I was pretty pumped about it.

CORY

RULES ROUND 1

BLASTERS

AR-L

SP-L   RL MICRO

TARGETS

BASS FISHING BATTLE. People that know me know I *love* fishing. I'm a fish kisser; it is what it is. So, this particular battle (most fish caught in the shortest amount of time) was extra fun for me.

CODY

REGULAR
1

DUDE PERFECT ROD
2

CANE POLE
3

DEEP SEA
4

HAND REEL
5

RADIO CONTROLLED BOAT
6

FASTEST TWO TIMES MOVE ON TO THE FINALE

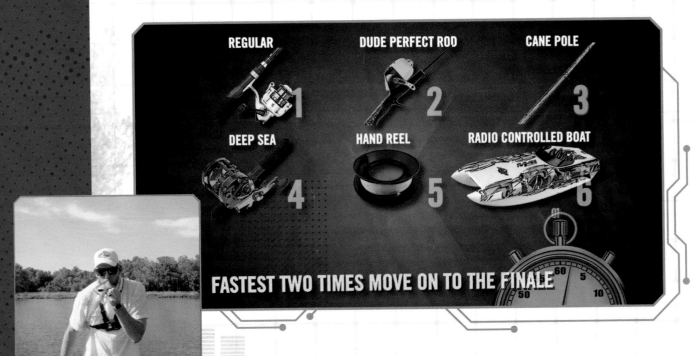

WHICH BATTLE WAS THE MOST DIFFICULT TO SET UP?

So far, the most difficult battles to set up would have to be the Nerf Floating Island Battle and the Helicopter Battleship Battle. The Nerf Floating Island Battle looked like a simple setup, but when you have to construct targets and hang branding signs in the middle of a lake without any of the items getting wet, it can be quite a struggle—especially when the Floating Island was incredibly slippery and the water was over our heads! We were definitely exhausted after that video shoot.

FUN FACT

For the Deep Sea Fishing Battle, we weren't just fishing offshore; we were *miles* off the coast—literally in the middle of the ocean! So not only did we have to wake up before the sun, but it took us a few hours to finally settle in a good fishing spot. Then, once we found our spot, we kept our fingers crossed because there is a lot of water out there and we had to hope that we were at a spot where the fish were. That battle took three full days to film!

The Helicopter Battleship Battle also was a tough setup, not because of the props, but this time because of the helicopters. Each team had one member go up in the copter with an item to drop on the game board, which meant the helicopter was constantly going up and down and teammates were switching back and forth. Then you had to take into account that, although you felt like you were looking straight down when you were in the air, the item that you were about to drop could go way off to one side, so trying to judge those angles was a challenge. Lastly, with the helicopters constantly in motion, we had to be aware of how much fuel we were using to make sure that the pilots had enough to get back to the airport.

TALL BEARD DROP ZONE

TWIN DROP ZONE

N2650

TEAM TWIN

TEAM TWIN

TEAM TALL BEARD

FUTURE BATTLES

It's hard to say what kind of battle we will do next. Even when the cameras are off, we find ourselves competing in normal everyday activities. We find inspiration in everything we do in terms of video ideas. It just depends if we have time to film it and if it will end up being something that our fans will enjoy. We love taking feedback from viewers, so if you think you have a great battle idea for us, go ahead and send us a note! In the meantime, you'll have to stay tuned to see what kinds of epic ideas we come up with next.

BATTLE TIME!

Now it's your turn! Use your own sports gear and household items to create all-out battles with your friends or family.

TRICK SHOT 93

NERF SLIP AND SLIDE BATTLE

Run! Jump! Aim! Blast! Crash!
Who can be the steadiest and most agile slider while shooting at targets?
A perfect battle for a hot summer day. **LET'S DO THIS!**

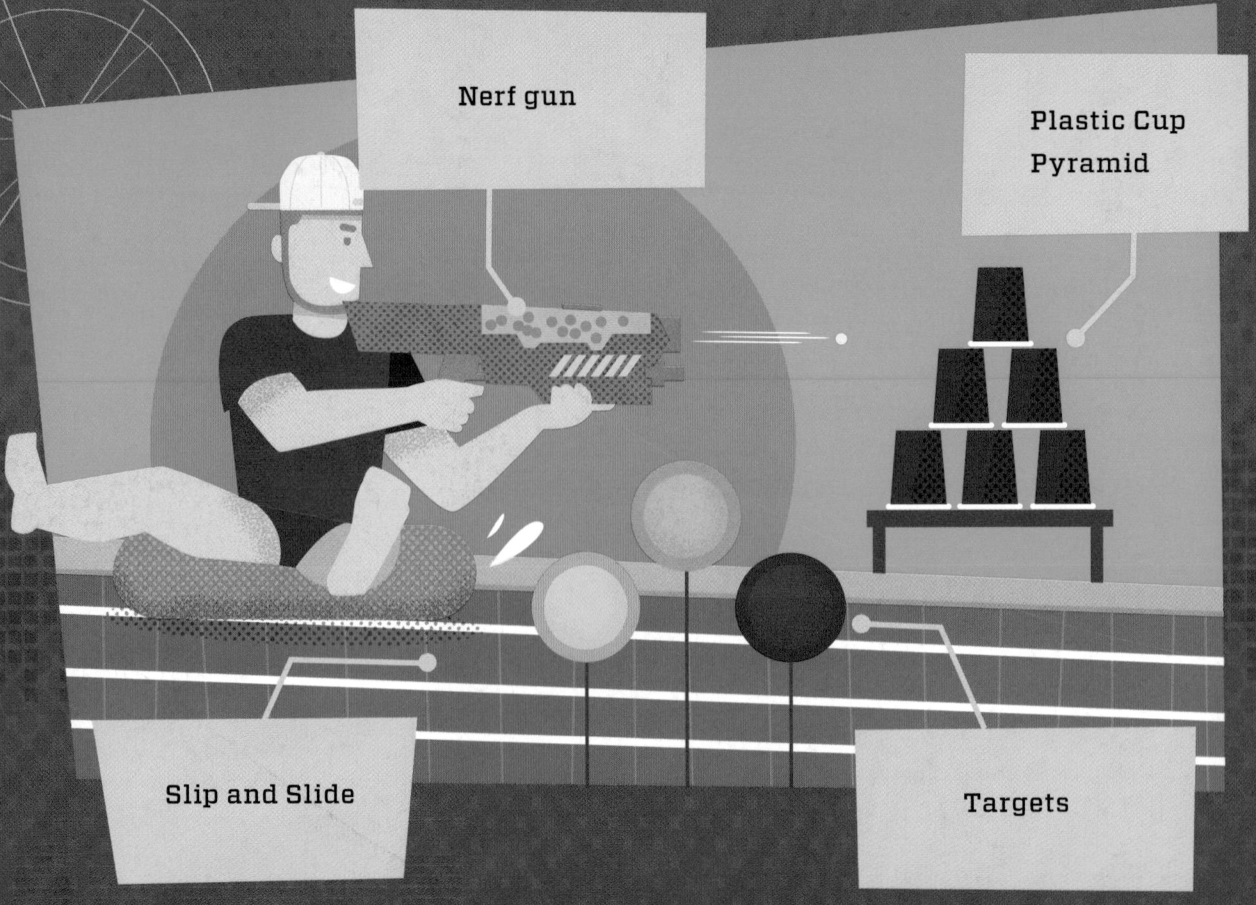

Nerf gun
Plastic Cup Pyramid
Slip and Slide
Targets

WHAT YOU'LL NEED:

- TWO OR MORE PLAYERS
- SLIP AND SLIDE
- WATER HOSE
- NERF GUNS
- PLASTIC CUPS
- TABLE
- BUCKET
- TARGETS OF DIFFERENT SIZES
- HILL (preferred, but not absolutely necessary)
- BABY OIL (optional for legendary-level sliding)
- SMALL INFLATABLE POOL (optional for safe landings)

GET STARTED

STEP 1

Position the slide going down a hill if you have one. Or run really, *really* fast before sliding. To avoid bruising your bum, place an inflatable pool at the bottom of the slide and fill it with water for a softer landing.

STEP 2

Place three targets of different sizes alongside the slide. You can use yard signs, stakes holding cardboard markers, snow stakes with paper plates attached—anything standing that can be hit. Make the smallest worth ten points, the medium-sized target worth five points, and the largest target worth three points.

NEXT PAGE

Just after the three targets, set up a table stacked with a pyramid of ten plastic cups. You get a point for every cup you knock over.

STEP 4

Set up a bucket on its side, facing the slide. Every shot in the bucket gets a point. (Tip: Use a brightly colored bucket to help you aim!)

STEP 5

Douse the slide and yourself with water. Use baby oil if you're feeling extra brave.

STEP 6

Make sure your Nerf Blaster is armed and ready.

Get a running start, then land on the slide ready to *FIRE AWAY!*

Play (k)

AirTrack Factory

STEP 8

Stay on the slide. Try to hit the targets. Stick the landing. Don't slide into a tree.

STEP 9   Tally your points. How many did you score?

FUN FACT

The world record for the longest Slip and Slide took place on October 16, 2015, in Amman, Jordan. The slide was 611.7 meters (2,006 feet and 10 inches). That's almost six football fields long!

How does a Slip and Slide work? Basically, all that slipperiness reduces friction. Friction is a force created when two surfaces rub against each other.

Friction slows down motion. A car won't go on forever because there is friction between the tires and the road. A soccer ball won't keep rolling because there is friction between the ball and the grass. However, a Slip and Slide has a couple of components that greatly reduce friction and allow users to go fast and far.

First, someone running up to a water slide has motion and energy. They will be stopped only if a force is applied to them to slow them down. Second, the slide is made of plastic. Smooth materials create less friction. Next, the slide is wet, which reduces the friction between the person and the plastic even more. The water acts as a lubricant. And if you add baby oil to the slide, there's even less friction to slow you down. The smooth, wet plastic reduces the force of friction to a very small amount and allows a person to keep most of their speed as they jump or dive onto it.

TRAMPOLINE CHARADES BATTLE

Jump into your next game of charades! Acting out the answers is a little trickier when you're bouncing up and down in the air. Yeah, you're gonna look pretty goofy, but so will your friends.

WHAT YOU'LL NEED:

- FIVE OR MORE PLAYERS
- TRAMPOLINE—THE BIGGER, THE BETTER
- TIMER
- PENS AND INDEX CARDS OR PAPER TO WRITE ANSWERS
- HAT OR BOWL
- SHARP, CREATIVE MINDS

GET STARTED

STEP 1

Select a judge and two or more teams.

COBY COTTON
TODAY'S JUDGE

dp | DUDEPERFECT

DUDEPERFECT

STEP 2

Choose three categories for the answers such as "activities," "phrases," or "movies."

STEP 3

Each team writes a set of answers for the other team. Be sure all answers make sense and can be acted out. Fold and place the slips of paper with answers into a cap.

NEXT PAGE

STEP 4

Decide which team goes first.

STEP 5

The first player picks four answers from the cap.

STEP 6

Set a timer for three minutes.

CLIPPING YOUR TOENAILS

STEP 7

Player jumps and acts out charades while other teammates guess. Score one point per correct guess. Remember to use your entire body—arms, legs, feet, face. Don't stop jumping!

COOL STUFF

If you want to see an absolute throwback, look up our video "Trampoline Edition Dude Perfect." We look young and weird and it's not our best video, but there are *lots* of trampolines involved.

PRO TIP

MASTERING THE TRAMPOLINE SHOT

1. Basic: Bounce up and down while making the shot.

2. Beyond Basic: Dunk while bouncing on a trampoline.

3. Advanced: The bouncing long ball. Bounce while launching a missile of a shot.

4. Expert: Do a flip and then make a basket.

STEP 8

The other team takes a turn by selecting four answers from the same category. Don't fall off the trampoline!

STEP 9

Play three rounds. Don't think with your feet; use your brain! Whoever scores the most points at the end wins.

2 POINTS

TEAM BATTLE CONSEQUENCE

COLD PIZZA SMOOTHIE

BONUS

Choose a Team Battle Consequence—something they're gonna hate. Like the losing team has to eat a cold microwavable pizza blended into a shake. *EWWWW!*

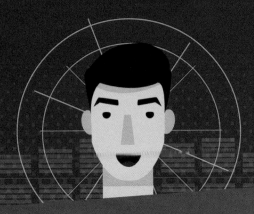

PRO TIP

HERE ARE A FEW HELPFUL TIPS WHEN PLAYING CHARADES.
Phrases can be sports-related like "Knock it out of the park" and "Down and out" or they can have something to do with food like "a piece of cake" and "driving me nuts."

 1. To show how many words are in the answer, hold up the correct number of fingers.

 2. Then to show which word you're working on, hold up another set of fingers. For example, "Riding a horse" gets three fingers raised. To have them guess the word *horse*, hold up three fingers again.

 3. If you want them to guess what the answer sounds like, cup your hand behind your ear.

 4. To show the length of the word, move your hands big or small as if you're measuring a fish.

 5. Find creative phrases and answers online.

Normally when you jump from the ground, your legs and body create a force upward. This force overcomes the force of gravity to move your body into the air. How high you can jump depends on how much force your leg muscles produce upward motion. Once in the air, your upward force decreases as gravity pulls you back down. But the bigger the upward force you create, the higher you will go!

When you fall down onto the trampoline, your weight and the force of gravity stretch out the springs in the trampoline. Now the springs hold all the energy from your jump. When the springs compress to their original position, they give you back the energy from your initial jump. Now you have two forces moving you upward: the energy from the springs and the energy from your body when you jump again. These two forces work together to launch you higher than just the force of jumping on your own could do.

A second force moving you upward: your body

Force of gravity

The force moving you upward: spring compression

95 GIANT DICTIONARY BATTLE

Who needs a pen when you can use paint? Make the biggest, messiest artwork you can think of! The bigger, the better.

GET STARTED

STEP 1

Set up your canvases and paint buckets outside on the ground. Lay your canvases flat or else the paint will drip down. #gravity

WHAT YOU'LL NEED:

- FIVE OR MORE PLAYERS
- WASHABLE PAINT—WASHABLE!
- OLD BROOMS
- OLD SHEET, PIECE OF PLYWOOD, GIANT CANVAS, OR ANYTHING LARGE ENOUGH TO PAINT ON
- HAT OR BOWL
- NOTEPAD AND PEN

STEP 2

Select two teams and pick a judge to be the guesser. Give the judge headphones with music playing so they can't hear. If you want to make them happy, play some '80s songs for them.

"IT'S LESS ABOUT WINNING, AND MORE ABOUT NOT LOSING."
—PANDA

PRO TIP

Trim the bristles of the brooms to make it easier to use them as giant paintbrushes.

STEP 3

Pick a category (an action, a person, a place, an animal, or a thing). Or make up your own category like animals doing stuff. (Example: A turtle driving a bus.) Each player writes down one thing from the category, folds the paper in two, and puts it in the hat or bowl.

STEP 4

The first team draws a word from the hat or bowl.

STEP 5   The team has one minute to discuss a strategy.

STEP 6   The judge starts the timer, and the team starts painting with the brooms. The judge starts guessing answers right away.

STEP 7   Stop the clock when the judge guesses the right answer.

STEP 8   The other team does the same steps.

STEP 9   The shortest time it takes the judge to guess the right answer is the winner.

DID YOU KNOW?

Playing games makes you smarter. No, really! Playing makes your brain stronger. As you play, you develop thinking skills because games exercise the areas in your brain that help you remember things and think through steps in complex processes. So, keep playing—no matter how old you are.

BIKE BATTLE

Make an epic course and become the most epic! We did the Dirt Bike Battle, but you can take out your regular bike to pedal to the finish. Do this one outside, away from traffic.

"THE COURSE IS EPIC. THE COMPETITION IS EPIC-ER. IT'S TIME TO BE THE EPIC-EST."

—TYLER

WHAT YOU'LL NEED:

- TWO OR MORE PEOPLE
- BICYCLES AND HELMETS (ALWAYS WEAR A HELMET!)
- A PLACE TO SET UP YOUR COURSE
- CONES OR PYLONS
- BALLS OR OTHER ITEMS TO USE AS OBSTACLES
- A TWO-BY-FOUR WOODEN BEAM
- NERF BLASTERS AND TARGETS
- TOY BOW AND SOFT, FOAM-TIPPED ARROWS WITH TARGETS
- STOPWATCH

GET STARTED

STEP 1 Set up your course. Position cones or something else to mark where to go.

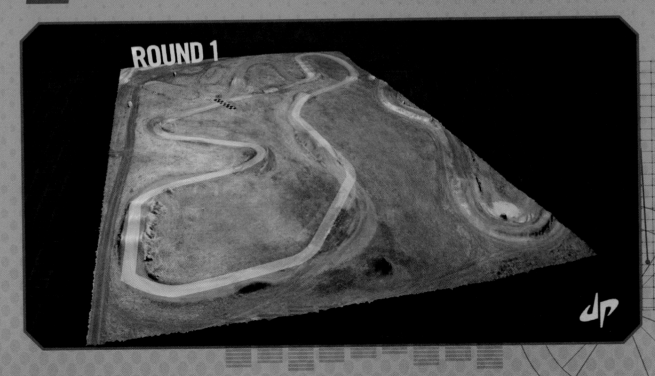

ROUND 1

There are more than four hundred world records in cycling. Some of the records involve the fastest times or farthest distances, while other record holders got very creative to earn their place in history. For example, Steve Gordon became a world record holder for "Longest Distance Cycling Backward on a Unicycle" when he . . . well . . . rode the longest distance cycling backward on a unicycle. He rode sixty-eight miles in Springfield, Missouri, on June 24, 1999.

STEP 2

Create obstacles and challenges on your course. Get creative! Drive around beach balls. Or have extra people roll or throw the balls across the path. (Gently, people! *Gently!*) Ride in a figure 8 around cones. Make a (small and safe!) bike jump. Have a low spot on your course? Fill it with water for a splashing puddle.

STEP 3

Set up the two-by-four wood beam—a.k.a. the "bridge of doom." Think of it as a bike balance beam. If your bike slips off of the balance beam, you have to go back and try again.

BANANA CORNER

STEP 5

Do the same thing with a toy bow and soft, foam-tipped arrows. Hitting the target means you finished the race!

STEP 4

Set up a place to shoot foam darts at a target. Riders have to hit the target before moving on.

STEP 6

Each player gets a turn to see how long it takes them to successfully finish the course. Use a stopwatch to time each person. Fastest time to finish wins!

PLASTIC GOLF CLUB BATTLE

PLASTIC GOLF CLUB BATTLE

Prepare for your own PGA tournament (Plastic Golf Association). As long as it's plastic, it's fantastic! The more colors, the better. Play inside or outside.

WHAT YOU'LL NEED:

- TWO OR MORE PLAYERS

- PLASTIC GOLF CLUBS AND PLASTIC BALLS

- PUTTING CUPS WITH FLAGS (preferably with bright, shiny colors)

- GOLF SWAG FOR COOLNESS FACTOR (Optional)

- SANDBOX OR SANDBAGS (optional: a sand trap makes your course above par)

- PAPER AND PENCIL

PGA ────────────── **RULES**

The rules of this battle are simple: After three holes of golf, the lowest score wins! To spice it up, come up with a reward for a hole in one!

STEP 1

Set up your course. Three holes. The more creative, the better. Use the stairs and hallways in your house or use anything you can outside: a friend's yard, neighborhood park, or even an empty parking lot.

① PAR 3

STEP 2

Place tees where you will start each hole. Make sure players know where the hole or cup is located.

② PAR 4

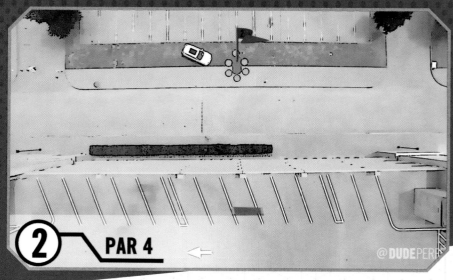

STEP 3

BE CREATIVE with where you place your greens. You're not likely to break anything with a plastic ball, so make players use walls, furniture, trees, or anything to bounce and bank their balls.

③ PAR 5

NEXT PAGE

STEP 4

Set up sand traps, if you can.

STEP 5

PLAY! Oh, and the only other rule in the PGA battle is you have to play the ball wherever it lies. (No do-overs.)

STEP 6

Keep score. After each hole, record how many shots it took each player to complete the hole. At the end of the round, add the scores from each individual hole and you'll get your total or gross score for the three holes.

CHALLENGE!

Construct your own putting green and small golf course with a few simple materials you already have around the house. Easy tip: position plastic cups or very small boxes on their sides to create a golf cup and tape them down using electrical tape or duct tape.

WHAT YOU'LL NEED:

- LARGE CARDBOARD BOX
- CLEAN YOGURT OR APPLESAUCE CUP
- SCISSORS OR RAZOR KNIFE
- ELECTRICAL OR DUCT TAPE, OR GLUE
- CONSTRUCTION PAPER
- STRAW

GET STARTED

STEP 1 With an adult's help, cut open a large cardboard box until it lays flat. If you want it to look like a golf course, paint it green and let it dry.

STEP 2 Trace the shape of the yogurt or applesauce cup onto the cardboard where you want the golf hole—or simply place a cup on its side and tape it down to hold it in place.

STEP 3 Cut out the circle, but make it a little smaller than the cup outline.

STEP 4 Glue the cup around the hole on the bottom of the cardboard. Place blocks or books to each side of the cup to form a platform. The cardboard will slope down around the cup.

STEP 5 Another option is to cut a box on the diagonal so that the cup is on a slight slope.

STEP 6 Make a flag with a triangle of colored paper and a straw and tape it to the inside of the cup or to the side if it's laying down.

FUN FACT

Just how likely are you to make a hole in one playing golf? The odds are 1 in 12,500. If you're a professional golfer, you have a 1 in 2,500 chance of making it.

DIZZY SPORTS BATTLE

Don't you just love it when you get off a roller coaster or the merry-go-round and you feel woozy? We took that feeling and made a game out of it. 'Round and 'round you go. Whether you can hit anything or not, nobody knows.

Basic rules: Have each person perform a dizzy punt, a dizzy baseball tee, and a dizzy golf swing. Total yardage wins!

F.A.D.P.D.S.B.

2 FINALISTS
TOTAL YDS WINS

GARRETT   CORY   COBY
TY   CODY

WHAT YOU'LL NEED:

- THREE OR MORE PLAYERS
- CONES
- FOOTBALL
- TWO BATS
- BLITZBALL, WIFFLE BALL, OR SOFTBALL
- BATTING TEE
- GOLF CLUB
- TENNIS BALL
- WATER BALLOONS
- PAPER AND PENCIL
- BALL OF STRING AND MEASURING TAPE
- AN EMPTY STOMACH

GET STARTED

STEP 1 Place one cone at your starting point. Set up your field with two lines of cones fanning out in a triangle from the starting cone. Place the cones about ten feet apart.

STEP 2 Place a football next to the starting cone.

FUN FACT

We've done a *lot* of dizzy competitions over the years. In case you're wondering, it does *not* get any easier. We get just as dizzy now as we ever have!

STEP 3

Stand behind the starting cone. With the tip of a bat touching the ground, press your forehead to the handle of the bat. Now spin around ten times. Keep your head down while you spin!

10 SPiNS

STEP 4

Release the bat and fall on your face. No, seriously, you're probably going to fall. Wear a helmet if you need to.

STEP 5 Pick up the football and throw it or kick it as far as you can onto the field. Measure the distance from the starting cone to the ball. If the distance is longer than your measuring tape, stretch the string from the cone to ball and use the measuring tape to determine the total length of the string. Write the distance on a score sheet.

STEP 6 Give each person a turn. Mark down the distance thrown. If the ball is thrown backward, the distance is a negative number.

NEXT PAGE

For the next round, give everyone a turn with a baseball on a tee and a bat except this time, go for thirteen spins before seeing how far each person can hit a softball, Blitzball, or Wiffle ball. Record everyone's distance. Yes, even if it's negative.

-8 INCHES

One more round! Feeling like throwin' up yet? Good. After sixteen spins, now try to swing a golf club at a tennis ball. Record each distance.

Add up each player's distance for all three rounds. Consult an accounting professional if you need to add a negative number. The two players with the highest score go to the final round.

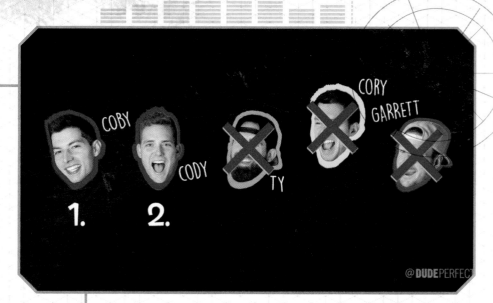

@DUDEPERFECT

STEP 10

LET'S DO THIS! It's time for the dizzy water balloon toss. This time, you're trying to hit the other person. At the count of ten, each player takes a turn spinning around ten times with their foreheads down on the end of the bat while the other person stands in place—without ducking. (Safety goggles recommended here.) Then fire! For the sake of safety and friendship, try to aim below their head. The first person to hit the other wins. If you both manage to hit each other, do it again until there's only one clear winner.

ALL SPORTS BOWLING BATTLE

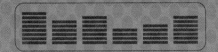

Turn a touchdown into a strike. Take a three-point shot and make ten. Have a gutter ball on the green. Kick for the win. When you're doing All Sports Bowling, you're taking the game to a whole other level. Well, actually several new levels!

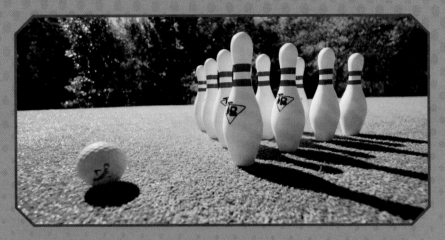

WHAT YOU'LL NEED:

- TWO OR MORE PEOPLE
- A SET OF BOWLING PINS (Ideally three sets: mini pins, regular, and oversized)
- EQUIPMENT FROM DIFFERENT SPORTS (such as football, soccer ball, basketball, putter and golf ball, Nerf gun—get creative here)
- PEN OR PENCIL
- HAT OR CUP

ADD THESE IF YOU HAVE THEM:

- TOY BOW AND ARROW SET (Not the real kind. C'mon!)
- CUE BALL AND POOL TABLE
- EXERCISE BALL

BASIC RULES

If only two people are battling, the person who knocks down the most pins over both rounds wins.

1. For games with three or more people, play two series of the first round.

2. The player with the most pins knocked down in each round will go to the second round.

FIRST ROUND

GET STARTED

STEP 1

Gather your equipment to figure out which sports you'll be incorporating. Write the name of each sport on a notecard or piece of paper. Then have each player pick two items from a hat or cup. Or if you have an old spinner from a board game, make categories on the spinner and let each player have a turn.

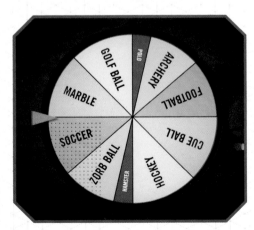

Arrange one set of bowling pins for the first player. Match the size of pins to the equipment.

FOR TOY BOW AND ARROW, use a regular set of bowling pins and set up outside. Shoot at the pins from fifty feet away.

FOR GOLF, use a set of small bowling pins.

STEP 3

Each player gets one try with their equipment. The player who knocks down the most pins wins that round. If two players tie with a strike, they will each draw for a new piece of equipment and bowl another round.

FOR BILLIARDS, use a set of small bowling pins and set up on a pool table, or set up a shot using a billiards stick and a cue ball on the ground.

BONUS

For fun, make a really *COOL* leaderboard.

SCOREBOARD

IN THE LEAD		CHOPPING BLOCK		
GARRETT	COBY	CORY	CODY	TYLER
9	7	5	3	1

PRO TIP

Make your own bowling pins with plastic bottles. Use two-liter bottles for large pins, liter-sized bottles for medium pins, and small eight-ounce bottles for small pins. Depending on the equipment you're using, fill the bottles halfway with water or rice to give them the weight of bowling pins.

GET STARTED

STEP 1

Set up pins on a basketball court, backyard, park, or even on your driveway.

STEP 2

Competitors will get one turn each with a football, a basketball, and a soccer ball to see how many pins they can knock down.

R1 R2
7

FINALE!

GET STARTED

STEP 1

Set up as many pins as you can. (We used 120 pins, so the more the merrier.)

STEP 2

Gather up to four different balls for four turns each. We used baseball, basketball, soccer ball, and football. Then allow each person to use them in the order of their choosing. (Just be sure to be consistent, allowing each person to have the same number of chances with the same equipment.)

STEP 3

Tally up everyone's score from all three rounds. The player with the most pins down wins.

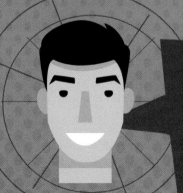

PRO TIP

If you don't have many pins, shoot from far away to make the shots more difficult.

Bowling is believed to have originated in ancient Egypt. Archeologists have found drawings showing a game similar to bowling on the walls of a royal tomb dated around 5,200 B.C. Miniature balls and pins were also found in an Egyptian child's grave from the same time period.

Believe it or not, there is a whole lot of science going on in bowling. But for now, let's just focus on one thing: trajectory. Trajectory is the curved path of an object that has been thrown or fired. So, with bowling, it's the path a ball takes that will deliver much more force as it hits the pins and will give the bowler a better shot at scoring.

DID YOU KNOW?

GIANT WARSHIP BATTLE

FIRE IN THE HOLE! Prepare to sink or swim in your very own personal battle of giant warships. Take down the other team with a barrage of water balloons. Paint balloons optional!

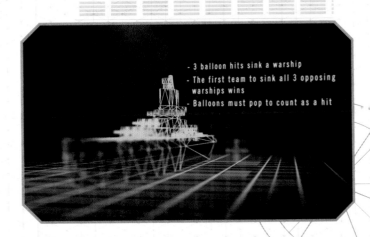

WHAT YOU'LL NEED:

- FOUR OR SIX PLAYERS, PLUS ONE JUDGE
- BALLOONS FILLED WITH WATER
- CONES, STRING, OR TAPE TO SHOW A TEAM'S "WATER"
- A TALL WALL PLACED BETWEEN TWO TEAMS
- A BOAT FOR EACH PLAYER— KAYAKS, CANOES, OR STAND-UP PADDLEBOARDS. BUT REALLY, WHO HAS SIX OF THOSE LYING AROUND? (Optional ideas: Sleds, large boxes you can fit in or cut-up cardboard pieces, old cushions you don't mind getting wet, pool floats)

BASIC RULES:

1. Three balloon hits sink a warship.
2. The first team to sink all opposing warships wins.
3. The balloon has to burst in order for the hit to count.

GET STARTED

STEP 1 Construct your wall.

STEP 2 Place boundary markers on the ground for each side to mark your team's water space. Mark out five rows and five columns with the cones, string, or tape. Label the columns A, B, C, D, and E. Label the rows 1, 2, 3, 4, and 5.

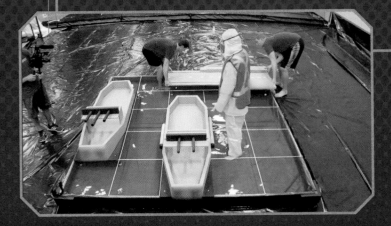

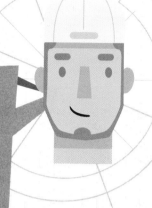

PRO TIP

HERE ARE SOME IDEAS FOR SETTING UP A WALL:

- Tape large boxes together and prop against tall cones or lawn chairs.

- Put a bed sheet over a swing set, a blanket over a clothesline, or drape a sheet over a volleyball net.

- Anybody in your neighborhood have a tall fence? That's perfect!

PRO TIP

Don't give away your position by being too loud. Being sneaky pays off!

STEP 3

Position your boats horizontal or vertical behind your barrier. Make sure you can't see the other team's water space.

STEP 4

Select a team to go first and then alternate teams with each throw. Each player gets one balloon toss per round. Players on the team not throwing have to lay on their boats and pray they don't get hit. (Ponchos optional.)

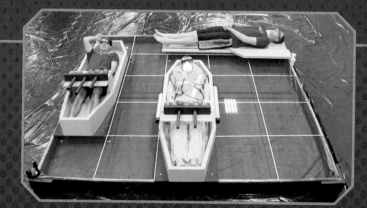

STEP 5

NEXT PAGE

The judge will call out "Hit!" or "Miss!" along with the square or cell where it landed. This will give players an idea of where to aim next.

STEP 6

If a player's warship is struck three times, they are sunk. The player has to immediately leave the water.

STEP 7

Last team with a player standing (or swimming) wins. Could be simple bragging rights or a reward. Or losers face the dreaded consequences. (For our battle, we duct-taped Cody and Cory to a giant post, but we don't recommend you try that at home.)

DID YOU KNOW?

Latex balloons are made of a combination of water and rubber, which is found beneath the bark of a rubber tree. Latex balloons will eventually decompose, although very slowly. Wildlife like birds will mistake pieces of latex balloons for food. If an animal eats a piece of latex, it can become sick or even die. A large piece of latex or a whole balloon will block the animal's digestive track so they can't eat real food and the animal will starve. Bottom line? Put trash in its place, and *SLAM DUNK THE JUNK*!

FUN FACT

For the first six years, we made our own props ourselves. More recently however, we added a few team members who have helped make many of the incredible sets and props you see on video, including the Giant Warship Battle. We love our team!

COOL STUFF

Brighten up the game! It's easy to create paint balloons. No, not real paint! Here are the ingredients for making homemade colorful water balloons.

WHAT YOU'LL NEED:

- WATER
- CORN STARCH
- EMPTY WATER BOTTLE
- FUNNEL
- WATER BALLOON
- WATER BALLOON NOZZLE
- FOOD COLORING

GET STARTED

STEP 1

Fill a mixing bowl with one cup of corn starch and one cup of water. Then mix in food coloring to create the color you want.

STEP 2

Pour paint into a water bottle using the funnel. Then attach the water balloon nozzle to the bottle.

STEP 3

Fill each balloon by attaching it to the nozzle and squeezing the paint from the bottle into the balloon. Tie the balloons tightly.

STEP 4

Play with your balloons. Wear goggles or sunglasses to protect your eyes from paint while playing.

SCORE!

NERF BLASTERS BATTLE

Hasta la vista, baby! Time to prove who's the best shot around. Grab your blaster and let's do this!

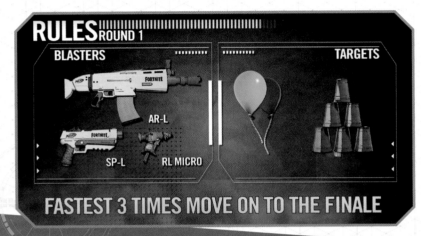

RULES Round 1

BLASTERS

AR-L

SP-L   RL MICRO

TARGETS

FASTEST 3 TIMES MOVE ON TO THE FINALE

WHAT YOU'LL NEED:

- TWO OR MORE PLAYERS
- NERF BLASTERS
  (with manual reload)
- TIMER
- TWENTY OR MORE
  16-OUNCE PLASTIC CUPS
- TABLE
- SMALL PLASTIC CONES
- BALLOONS FILLED WITH
  HELIUM
- LARGE HULA-HOOP
- CUSHIONS OR A MATTRESS
- BULL'S-EYE TARGET

GET STARTED

STEP 1

Set up your course. Ours was rather elaborate, but you can make a course by getting creative and letting your imagination run a little wild. One of the basic shots to set up is to build a pyramid of plastic cups on a table. This is your first target.

STEP 2

The next target uses balloons. Fill balloons with helium and then tie them with string to chairs or other furniture several feet away from each other. If you don't have helium, tape the balloons to the wall or furniture, or hang them by a string from the ceiling.

STEP 3

Hang the hoop from the ceiling or wall so you can jump through it. If you don't have a hoop big enough, place a barricade across the path to jump over.

As funny as it is to talk after inhaling helium, it can actually be dangerous—even lethal! That's because when you inhale helium, it replaces the oxygen you would normally be breathing. As you breathe, your lungs are only getting helium. Inhaling helium can also cause dizziness, nausea, and lightheadedness.

DID YOU KNOW?

STEP 4

Set up the bull's-eye nearby your hoop or barricade. You will need to shoot the target in mid-jump.

STEP 5

Place the cushions or mattress just beyond the hoop or barricade to land on.

STEP 6

Make a path with plastic cones to each target.

STEP 7

PLAY! Set the timer for twenty seconds for each player. The player must run through the course and shoot as many cups as possible, shoot as many balloons as possible, then hit the bull's-eye while jumping through the hoop or over the barricade. Hitting the bull's-eye earns fifteen points. Make sure you have a round left in your blaster!

STEP 8

If a player doesn't make it in twenty seconds, they're disqualified and have to try again.

STEP 9

The player with the most points is the *WINNER.*

CHAPTER TWELVE

STEREOTYPES

WE ALL KNOW THEM. The guy who catches everything but a fish. Someone who drinks a gallon of water at the gym. The over-friendly waiter. The overprotective mother at the beach. Stereotypes are so much fun because there are so many of them out there!

For us, the fun started when Cory thought it'd be funny to show all the different types of pickup basketball players. From Mr. Excuses to the Imaginary Dunker to the Misses-All-Game-but-Banks-in-a-Three-for-the-Win Guy. Once we did it, we knew we had to keep doing more videos like that!

From camping to skiing, shopping to Super Bowl parties, we love poking fun at all the various types of people we see (and at ourselves). Stereotypes are funny because there's often some truth in them. For every driver you see, every hunter you can't see (camo), and every Christmas gathering you can't get out of, here are some of our favorite stereotypes!

SPORTS

From the soft greens to the hard asphalt, they will come. From the snowy slopes to the pitching mound, they will come. All shapes and sizes to invade your favorite sport . . .

PICKUP BASKETBALL

Every court has them. You know who you are.

1	**MR. EXCUSES** "Ooh, just got a massage. A little loose."
2	**THE FOOTBALL PLAYER** "This is street ball, man."
3	**THE PLAYER COACH** "Run Banana Swirl play!"
4	**THE OLD GUY** "I met Wilt Chamberlain . . ."
5	**THE IMAGINARY DUNKER** "I'm gonna go two hands."
6	**THE FOUL GUY** "Respect the call."
7	**THE TALL GUY THAT SHOOTS 3'S** "Post up! You're 6-6!"
8	**THE PANTS GUY** "It's 110 out here."
9	**MR. FREEZE** "They, like, attacked me."
10	**MR. SHOULDA MADE THE LEAGUE** "A couple of teams called . . ."

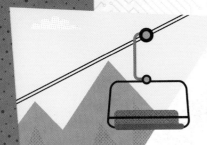

SKIING

To boldly ski where no skier has ever gone before . . .

1	THE SNOW SPRAYER "Woohoo!"
2	THE CHAIRLIFT STRUGGLERS "Gotta let it go, man!"
3	THE NOOB "What? Do you mean I need my skis?"
4	THE SPEED DEMON "See you later, hosers."
5	CHAIRLIFT HECKLERS "Hey, you should probably quit skiing and pick up sledding."
6	MR. INJURY PRONE "I've got, like, a hangnail."
7	THE SLOPE SITTERS "Hey, you got sandwiches? I say we eat here."
8	MR. EXCUSES "I cannot ski with a group of eight."
9	DO IT FOR THE GRAM "It's everything I dreamed it would be."
10	THE TRAILBLAZER "Dude, if the run has a name, we're not doing it."

GOLF

Why didn't the golfer get his homework done?
He was puttering around.

1	**SAND-TRAPPED GUY** "Tough lie."
2	**THE SHADOW GUY** "Your head is on my ball."
3	**MR. EXCUSES** "A fly just landed on my ball as I swung."
4	**THE TEE-BOX TALKER** "Hey, Cody, what'd you get on your last hole?"
5	**MR. MOOD SWING** "I hate this sport!"
6	**THE BALL HUNTER** "It's a Wilson 4!"
7	**THE THAT'S-PLAYABLE GUY** "That was smart golf."
8	**THE INSISTS-ON-TRYING-A-HAPPY-GILMORE-SHOT GUY** "I gotta do it. I do it every time."
9	**THE TOO-MANY-PRACTICE-SWINGS GUY** "Any day now."
10	**PGA RULE ENFORCER** "You ever read a rule book?"
11	**UNTRUSTWORTHY SCORE KEEPER** "Yeah, yeah—double bogey. That's what I was going to say."

SOFTBALL

There's always next week.
Or the week after that.
Or the week after that.

1	**I-GOT-IT GUY** "I got it, I got it!"
2	**NERVOUS NELLY** "You said we were playing softball—these things are hard as a rock."
3	**THE OUTRAGEOUS UMPIRE** "Woohhooo!!!"
4	**SIR SLIDES-A-LOT** "You never know—some of these guys have cannons out here."
5	**MR. STEEL TRAP MEMORY** "According to my calculations, he's due for a ground out to third."
6	**THE BORDERLINE, ILLEGAL, SEMI-FROWNED-UPON, LAST MINUTE CALL TO YOUR BUDDY WHO MAY OR MAY NOT BE ON AN MLB ROSTER** "Hey, I'm putting you down on the roster as Bris Cryant."
7	**MR. ACCESSORIES** "What is that?"
8	**THE SNACK GUY** "I have bacon seeds, ranch seeds, bacon ranch seeds."
9	**TEAM MOM** "Hey, guys. I know you're bummed. Losing 13–0 again is really hard. Look on the bright side, though, because we have gushers and orange slices."

ACTIVITIES

No matter where you go, there they are. From commuting to work, to celebrating holidays, to working out at the gym—these are the people who stand out.

DRIVING

"GET OUT OF MY WAY!" Some of us spend a lot of time in our cars. Naturally there are all types of drivers on the road. Even some famous ones.

1	**WING-MAN** "Stay awake! Safety first!"
2	**MR. LIVES IN HIS CAR** "You never know when you've gotta sizzle a patty."
3	**THE BLACK HOLE** "Oh, dude, that's a perfectly good chicken sandwich!"
4	**THE RACER** "Wanna take these guys?"
5	**BUMPER STICKER STEVE** "It's mine! I like to draw attention!"
6	**THE PARKING POLICEMAN** "Oh my gosh, are you serious? You are over the line!"
7	**LEAVES-IT-IN-DRIVE LARRY** "Dude, your car is running away!"
8	**THE DAD INSPECTOR** "Where's your registration and inspection sticker? You gonna get this washed anytime soon?"

CHRISTMAS

"Dashing through the snow

With five Dudes on a sleigh

O'er the fields we go

Laughing all the way . . ."

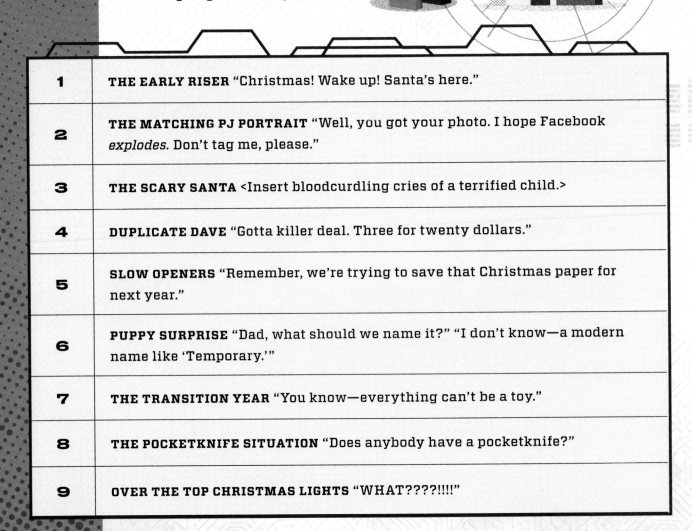

1	**THE EARLY RISER** "Christmas! Wake up! Santa's here."
2	**THE MATCHING PJ PORTRAIT** "Well, you got your photo. I hope Facebook *explodes.* Don't tag me, please."
3	**THE SCARY SANTA** <Insert bloodcurdling cries of a terrified child.>
4	**DUPLICATE DAVE** "Gotta killer deal. Three for twenty dollars."
5	**SLOW OPENERS** "Remember, we're trying to save that Christmas paper for next year."
6	**PUPPY SURPRISE** "Dad, what should we name it?" "I don't know—a modern name like 'Temporary.'"
7	**THE TRANSITION YEAR** "You know—everything can't be a toy."
8	**THE POCKETKNIFE SITUATION** "Does anybody have a pocketknife?"
9	**OVER THE TOP CHRISTMAS LIGHTS** "WHAT????!!!!"

FISHING

Good things come to those who bait.

1	**CAPTAIN HOOK**	"What kind of bait is this?"
2	**MR. NO TOUCHIE**	"Nah-uh. No way."
3	**THE OVERESTI-BAITER**	"Big bait catches big fish."
4	**MR. EXCUSES**	"Way too nice weather. Always fish better in the rain."
5	**CATCHES EVERYTHING BUT A FISH**	"That's a Hot Pocket!"
6	**THE FISH HEAR EVERYTHING GUY**	"Shh! Sign language!!"
7	**THE TREE MAGNET**	"Ouch."
8	**THE LINE CROSSER**	"You are seriously out of control."
9	**LUCKY-LURE LARRY**	"I went to lure school, and I just happen to have one of my specialties."

HUNTING

Get out your camo. Put on your waders. Grab your crossbow. Pick out your stand. Bring your dog. Wait . . . what are we hunting again?

#	
1	**WHITE LIAR GUN BUYER** "How much? Oh, three or four hundred . . ."
2	**NOISY NED** "Don't move—huge buck! Nope, he's running away."
3	**BUY-IT-ALL BOB** "Donkey butter? Is it even donkey season?"
4	**DECOY OVERLOAD** "Do you see any major gaps I need to fill?"
5	**THE NOOB** "Oh, somebody left apple juice . . ."
6	**THE SKY BLASTER** "No, you weren't close at all!"
7	**BLIND NAPPERS** <Zzzzzzzz.>
8	**SAFETY-ORANGE SAMMY** "My bottom half looks very quail-like."
9	**THE SNACK MASTER** "You brought eggs? And bacon?"
10	**MR. HARDCORE** "Deer smell toothpaste from a mile away."

CAMPING

Just a heads up, this next section is a little in-tents.

1	**S'MORES WARS** "Medium rare with a golden crust."
2	**THE BEAR GRYLLS WANNABE** "Bruce is weak. I'm havin' lizard."
3	**MOSQUITO DEFENDER** "Not today, skeeters. I'm not taking any chances."
4	**THE NATURE EXPERT** "Well I'll be. A Montezuma Bald Cyprus. We meet again."
5	**THE CAMPFIRE SINGER** "Oh, you know what? I brought my guitar!"
6	**MR. WHAT WAS THAT?** "That could've been a Sasquatch."
7	**THE GLAMPER** "Now *this* is camping."
8	**THE GADGET GUY** "Am I the only one who brought a portable air conditioner?"

PLACES

Eating. Shopping. Watching a movie. Working out. We all have places to go. And each place has lots of unique characters.

MOVIE THEATER

Some think all you do in a movie theater is watch a film. Nope!

1	**THE OBNOXIOUS LAUGHER** "HAHAHAHHAHAHAAHAHAHA."
2	**THE MOOCHER** "I just want a taste. Not even a bite. Just a taste."
3	**THE SEAT SAVER** "See? We have the second row too."
4	**MR. JUMPY** "It's just a movie, it's just a movie. Don't freak out."
5	**THE SMUGGLER** "Nothing to see here."
6	**THE BUTTERY-POPCORN GUY** "Get it real soggy like . . ."
7	**THE LOUD EATER** *<Crackle. Chomp. Slurp.>*
8	**THE TEXTER** "Take it outside!"
9	**THE SUPER-FAN** "Sorry, guys. I misplaced my wand. *Again.*"
10	**THE BATHROOM CHAMPION** "I told you not to get two drinks."
11	**THE SNOOZER** "I've been waiting three months for this, man . . ." (Five minutes later: "Zzzzzz.")

GYM

It's time to pump you up!

1	**MR. EXCUSES** "It is *way* too early to work out."
2	**THE NO-IDEA-WHAT-I'M-DOING GUY** "Leg weights—yeah, buddy."
3	**THE SCREAMER** "AAAAAAAAARRRRRRRGGGGGGGGHHHHH!"
4	**THE MIRROR MAGNET** "Ooh—that's firm."
5	**THE GALLON-OF-WATER GUY** <*Glug, glug, glug . . .*>
6	**THE TREADMILL SPRINTER** "What's this guy doing?"
7	**THE PROTEIN GUY** "Protein goes into the mouth and goes into the muscle."
8	**THE SELFIE GUY** #BeastMode
9	**TALKATIVE TIMMY** "Oh, hey, what's up? I saw you here last week."

BEACH

The buff and the beautiful. The bold and the bronze. The breeze and the boats. There's a lot of things you can find at the beach, including this selection of people.

1	**HOT SAND** "Oww-oww-oww—my feet are on fire! Save yourself!"
2	**MR. SUNSCREEN** "When you match the color of the sand, that's when you know you have enough on."
3	**THE SURFER BROS** "You know—you're going to get smoked out here. That's just part of the job description when you're a couple of thrashers like us."
4	**SANDCASTLE CAPTAIN** "I don't want anyone within thirty meters of this perimeter."
5	**THE DIVING-CATCH GUY** "Nice toss!!!!"
6	**THE JUMPING PICTURE** "Can you take just one more? Just one?"
7	**THE RAINY DAY** "It's really not that bad."
8	**THE SOUVENIR GUY** "Customized knives with your name on it?"
9	**THE PRANK BROS** "Shark! Shark!"
10	**MR. BURY ME** "Guys! Bury me!"
11	**THE RUNNER** "Morning, boys!"

RESTAURANT

Can't we just eat in peace? But no way—these people aren't going to let you have a normal dining experience.

1	**THE AMBITIOUS REFILLER** "Wow? More? Already?"
2	**MR. NO MANNERS** "Do you think this is athlete's foot?"
3	**THE OVER-FRIENDLY WAITER** "How are we? My best buddies. Don't blink, I got your drinks."
4	**THE FAKE-NAME GUY** "Katniss Everdeen, party of two."
5	**CLUMSY WAITER** "Oops . . ."
6	**THE ANNOYING-MUSIC MAN** "Just give me a kiss!"
7	**THE PHONE ADDICTS** "Hey coach, what are you getting to eat? Sorry, I'll just text you."
8	**BIG PRICE, SMALL PORTION** "The 'Shrimps Platter' actually comes with two."
9	**THE OBNOXIOUS BIRTHDAY CELEBRATION** "I just wanted the free dessert."

GROCERY STORE

Deciding which lane to use for checkout. Deciding to not get a shopping cart or basket. Shopping when you're hungry. Here are all the wonderful types of people who shop at a grocery store.

1	**THE AISLE BLOCKADE** "Shopping cart confusion and roadblock on aisle three near the SpaghettiOs and salsa."
2	**HUNGRY SHOPPER** "Just gotta stick to the list . . ."
3	**CHATTY CHECKOUT** "Funny story: I actually lived next to triplets. Twice."
4	**PRODUCE INSPECTOR** "Ripeness test. Saw this on Pinterest."
5	**MR. EXPIRATION DATE** "Just looking for fresh milk!"
6	**THE LOST GUY** "They do not have dried cilantro in this store!"
7	**THE ONE-TRIP MASTER** "Two trips? Yeah right."
8	**THE GUY THAT FORGETS THE ONLY IMPORTANT THING** "Oh, dude, I knew I forgot something."
9	**THE CART RIDER** "Woohoo! Yeehaw!"
10	**THE SAMPLE THIEVES** "Free samples. One per customer."
11	**MR. CARTLESS** "Just grabbin' one thing."

QUARANTINE

Stuck inside.

Staying sanitized.

Sharing selfies.

Zooming besties.

1	**THE BINGE WATCHERS** "The entire Harry Potter series is even better upside down."	
2	**THE NEW-HOBBY GUY** "I always knew I was a LEGOs guy!"	
3	**MR. HOMEMADE MASK** "It fits pretty good—I just forgot to make eye holes."	
4	**HANDSHAKES IN 2021 BE LIKE** . . . "Stay safe out there."	
5	**AT-HOME HAIRCUT** "Yep. It's time."	
6	**NEW HOMESCHOOL PARENTS** "So . . . photosynthesis . . ."	
7	**QUARANTINE BIRTHDAY** "Happy birthday to me. Happy birthday to me."	
8	**THE HOARDER** "Pretty good TP tower you got going on there."	
9	**THE TIKTOK DAD** "Man—I nailed that one."	
10	**MR. INSTAGRAM CHALLENGE** "See a dog, post a dog!"	
11	**THE NEW-PUPPY PURCHASE** "I cannot believe we just did that."	

SPORTS FANS

Our fun usually involves sports of some kind. Sports on the television. Sports on video games. Games out of sports. Sports-related parties. There are so many ways to enjoy sports without even sweating!

1	**MADDEN** "So there I was, dominating Madden . . ."
2	**MR. EXCUSES** "I cannot play on the left side of the couch."
3	**THE NOOB** "What's the pass button?"
4	**THE REPLAY GUY** "Make cool plays and you can watch them on replay too."
5	**THE PHONE GUY** "Are you even playing?"
6	**THE CHEATER** "It's like you know what I'm doing."
7	**MR. GOIN' FOR IT** "You don't punt on fourth down."
8	**THE TRASH TALKER** "You're literally the worst ever!"
9	**THE HUMAN CONTROLLER** "Spin move. Hurdle."
10	**THE POWER-BUTTON PUSHER** "Up 24–0. Guess it's just not your day, Mr. Undefeated."
11	**THE CREATE-A-PLAYER** "Seventy-six on strength? I'm already more than that. I'm a ninety-nine."
12	**THE ONE-PLAY GUY** "Works every time."

FANTASY FOOTBALL

You know these people. You've seen them in your league. Maybe you're even one of them!

1	**THE HOMER** "How 'bout them Cowboys?"
2	**MR. KNOW IT ALL** "According to my calculations, I've got this wrapped up."
3	**THE RIDICULOUS TRADER** "I'm gonna up the stakes. I'm going to slip you this twenty. And my two scrubs."
4	**THE COMMISH** "New rule—we're going to have no running backs."
5	**THE TRAITOR** "Take this jersey off!"
6	**MR. AUTO DRAFT** "Haha—auto pick, sucker."
7	**MR. FEELING** "I've got a great feeling."
8	**THE FULL-TIMER** "I had four drafts last night."
9	**THE DOCTOR** "Bet he gets injured."
10	**THE LAZY COACH** "I noticed you had three empty slots on your roster."
11	**THE TRASH TALKER** "You're going to toast all his bread and put it back in the package?"

MARCH MADNESS

Yes! You've locked your brackets and are ready to go! You've picked UNT New College at Frisco to go all the way. That's how you do it!

1	**ULTIMATE-SETUP GUY** "Oh! What a shot!"
2	**SNEAKY WATCHERS** "Dude, last-second shot!"
3	**MASCOT PICKER** "I can't pick the Blue Devils. My dad works at a church."
4	**EMOTIONAL PICKER** "Well I had an uncle that went to Tech—never did like him . . ."
5	**THE FOOTBALL SCHOOL** "If this was football, we would be *killing* them!"
6	**MR. EXCUSES** "Wow, refs really lost me that one."
7	**THE DUKE DILEMMA** "And South Carolina coming out on top sending Duke home early."
8	**NO-BRAINER** "Women's bracket?" "UConn."
9	**ONE CRYING MOMENT** "Are you seriously crying right now?"
10	**LONGSHOT-FAN CONNECTION** "So you're a Wildcat because your almost-brother almost went to Kentucky?"

SUPER BOWL PARTY

The food. The commercials. The commercials about the food. The halftime show. Ah, yes, it's Super Bowl time!

1	**THE SUPERSTITIOUS FANS** "Hey—should we switch pants?"
2	**THE PARTY FOUL** "Oh . . . my bad, guys."
3	**THE BITTER FANS** "We gifted you that opportunity!"
4	**THE HORRIBLE HOST** "I forgot the food, guys."
5	**MR. COMMERCIALS** "Guys! Guys! Commercials are on! We should totally rate them! Most funny to least funny!"
6	**THE PARTY HOPPER** "Glad I can make it. Sorry I'm late. Actually, gotta run. Let's take a quick pic. *Party!*"
7	**THE PARTY CRASHER** "Dude, who is that guy?"
8	**BRINGS NOTHING . . . BUT TAKES EVERYTHING** "This is great!"
9	**WHERE-IS-MY-CUP GUY** "No worries—I'll just get a new one."
10	**THE UNWANTED VEGGIE TRAY** "We should have gotten here earlier."

STEREOTYPES Q&A WITH THE DUDES

WHICH STEREOTYPE BEST MATCHES EACH OF THE GUYS?

GARRETT	The New-Hobby Guy from Quarantine Stereotype or all of the Mr. Excuses
CORY	The Slacker from Camping Stereotypes or the Foul Guy from Basketball Stereotypes
COBY	The Loud Eater from Movie Theater Stereotypes
CODY	The Tall Guy that Shoots 3's from Basketball Stereotypes
TY	The Smuggler from Movie Theater Stereotypes

HOW DO WE COME UP WITH THE FINAL LIST OF STEREOTYPES?

The character ideas come pretty quickly, but deciding how to make each character over the top, visual, and extra funny is the tough part.

WILL THERE EVER BE AN ENTIRE VIDEO FEATURING THE RAGE MONSTER?

Maybe we'll do a "Best of the Rage Monster" video one day. That'd be one loud video.

WHAT ARE OUR FAVORITE STEREOTYPE VIDEOS SO FAR?

GARRETT	Hunting Stereotypes.
CORY	Pickup Basketball.
COBY	I loved the original Pickup Basketball Stereotypes. I was proud of how we did it. Another favorite is the Skiing Stereotypes. That was a lot of fun. They all have a special place in my heart. We work as hard on those as anything we've done. We have a really high bar set for how they turn out. There's a lot of stuff we try that never makes it to the final cut. Some of my bad acting thankfully doesn't make it to the final cut.
CODY	Beach Stereotypes.
TY	Golf Stereotypes was so relatable. Driving Stereotypes was fun. We worked with Dale Earnhardt Jr., and he was awesome. He was the first celebrity to be in a stereotypes video. We had a blast with him.

FUN FACT

When Ty raged the basketball court during "Grocery Store Stereotypes," that court was going to have to be replaced anyways. We had recently had an internal office flood that completely warped the court (you couldn't tell on camera). So, we took advantage of a tough situation and decided to pickax what looked like a perfectly good court. To be clear, as basketball fans, it still hurt each of our souls.

HAVE WE BEEN SURPRISED BY ANY OF THE STEREOTYPES?

The Christmas Stereotypes Rage Monster turned out better than expected. Getting to body slam the Christmas tree—that was a good payoff. The car we destroyed in "Driving Stereotypes"—first time we ever did anything like that. We ended up buying the car from one of Garrett's buddies. Thing barely turned on. We bought it for $1,500 (we overpaid).

Every Rage Monster scene is funny on camera and priceless in person. We always try to do it in one take (understandably). Whether it's a flamethrower or a flying pot of chili, the result is amazing (but also expensive).

PRO TIP

Sure, the Rage Monster is funny to watch on screen, but no one likes a Rage Monster in real life.

ANATOMY OF THE RAGE MONSTER

The Rage Monster was born during our first stereotype video, "Pickup Basketball Stereotypes." He was simply the guy who gets mad during a game and punts the ball away. But Ty had fun being this character, and we had fun watching him. So, we kept including him in future stereotype videos. And you could say things escalated quickly. Now filming a Rage Monster scene is an all-day affair, and it often costs a *lot* of money. But people have come to expect big things from this part of the video, and by golly, we're going to give the people what they want!

RAGE MONSTER STATS (SO FAR)

1 SECOND
SHORTEST RAGE
(GOT TAZED)

22
ITEMS USED
TO DAMAGE
SOMETHING ELSE

20
TOTAL RAGES

30.6 SECONDS
AVERAGE RAGE

1 MINUTE AND 26 SECONDS
LONGEST RAGE

15%
A BOWLING BALL IS USED

20%
A VEHICLE IS USED

35%
AN ITEM IS BATTED

85%
AN ITEM IS THROWN

TORCH • FIREWOOD • TREE • TRACTOR • SWORD • KNIFE • JACK • PICKAX • SLEDGEHAMMER • PAINTBALL GUN • SPRAY PAIN • BOWLING BALL • GOLF CART • PRY BAR • BULLDOZER • CHA • CK • WEIGHTS • SKILL SAW • BASEBALL BAT • BLOW TORC • OF CHILI

CHAPTER THIRTEEN

BUCKET LIST

BUCKET LIST ITEMS are not your average, everyday, ordinary experiences. They are special. They are rare. They feel like magic. They are the "I hope I get to do this thing before I kick the bucket" kinds of things—hence the name "Bucket List." They're like, *really cool.*

Because they are rare and special—and often extremely difficult or challenging in some way—we've done only one Bucket List video so far. "Bucket List: Aircraft Carrier" launched on January 13, 2020. However, we have plans to do a lot more! Maybe launching a rocket with NASA, scuba diving in the Great Barrier Reef, and going to the North Pole—just to name a few! You'll have to stay tuned to our YouTube channel in order to see what's next!

BUCKET LIST: AIRCRAFT CARRIER

Commander Ron Flanders of the United States Navy called us to let us know some good news: we got the green light to spend three days on an aircraft carrier, the USS *Nimitz*, in the Pacific Ocean!

The USS *Nimitz* is no joke; it's about the length of three football fields. It houses six thousand people and about sixty jets. It's HUGE!

X 10

Going on an aircraft carrier is cool on its own, but we made a list of ideas that, if we could do them *on the ship,* it would be insane. After laughing, Commander Flanders said he'd work with us to see how many of those bucket list items we could pull off. What was on our list? Glad you asked.

MASTER LIST

USS NIMITZ

☐ CATCH A FISH
☐ FLY A REMOTE CONTROLLED JET
☐ HIT GOLF BALLS OFF THE DECK
☐ GRILL AT SEA
☐ MAKE A TRICK SHOT
☐ WAKEBOARD BEHIND THE SHIP
☐ DRIVE THE SHIP
☐ FLY IN A JET
☐ HOT TUB
☐ SHOOT OFF A JET
☐ PLAY BASKETBALL ON THE DECK

Some of these items we got the green light for, but there's never a guarantee it's going to happen. Like make a trick shot. Or catch a fish. So, we had seven deep sea fishing rods going off the back deck of the carrier—perhaps the first time in history that's ever happened. Then a while later someone yelled, "Fish on!" We went running, and Ty reeled it in. And when we were granted permission to try a basketball trick shot, Ty nailed it!

FINAL RESULTS

We managed to complete ten out of eleven of the items from our bucket list. Not bad!

FLY A REMOTE CONTROLLED JET

HOT TUB

GRILL AT SEA

MAKE A TRICK SHOT

DRIVE THE SHIP

CATCH A FISH

FLY IN A JET

SHOOT OFF A JET

PLAY BASKETBALL ON THE DECK

HIT GOLF BALLS OFF THE DECK

WAKEBOARD BEHIND THE SHIP

The only bucket list item we weren't allowed to cross off was wakeboarding behind the ship. The captain said it was too dangerous. Even we have to obey the rules.

But we've gotta say—one of the coolest parts of checking off our bucket list was watching Cody fly in an F-18 Hornet with the Blue Angels—one of his personal dreams coming true. Tyler flew alongside in another jet while the rest of us watched our Blue Angel Bucket List Bros reach speeds of seven hundred miles per hour!

How'd they do? Well . . . we made a very special scoreboard for this one.

PUKE CHART

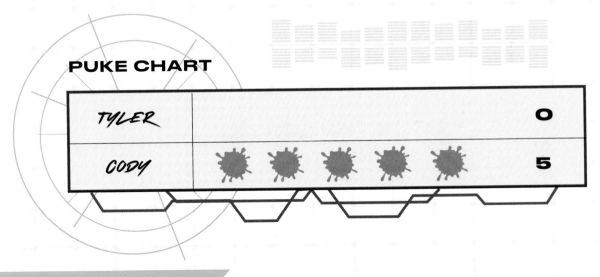

TYLER		0
CODY	🔵🔵🔵🔵🔵	5

WHERE IT ALL HAPPENED

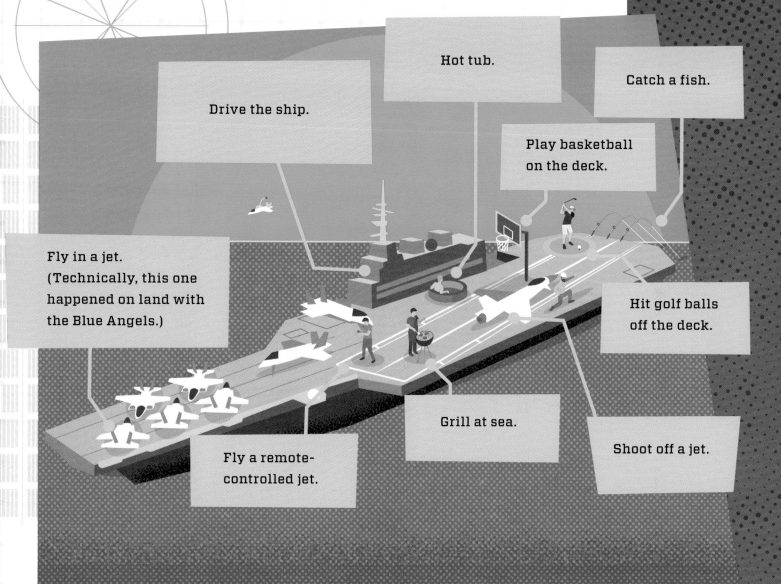

Hot tub.

Catch a fish.

Drive the ship.

Play basketball on the deck.

Fly in a jet. (Technically, this one happened on land with the Blue Angels.)

Hit golf balls off the deck.

Grill at sea.

Fly a remote-controlled jet.

Shoot off a jet.

COOL STUFF

When filming, we used biodegradable golf balls to not litter in the ocean.

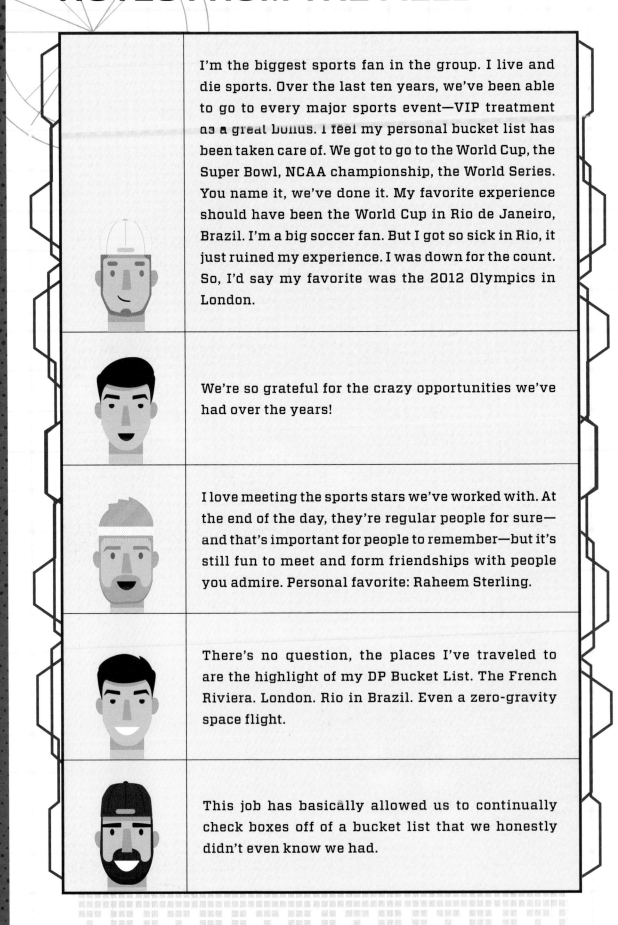

I'm the biggest sports fan in the group. I live and die sports. Over the last ten years, we've been able to go to every major sports event—VIP treatment as a great bonus. I feel my personal bucket list has been taken care of. We got to go to the World Cup, the Super Bowl, NCAA championship, the World Series. You name it, we've done it. My favorite experience should have been the World Cup in Rio de Janeiro, Brazil. I'm a big soccer fan. But I got so sick in Rio, it just ruined my experience. I was down for the count. So, I'd say my favorite was the 2012 Olympics in London.

We're so grateful for the crazy opportunities we've had over the years!

I love meeting the sports stars we've worked with. At the end of the day, they're regular people for sure— and that's important for people to remember—but it's still fun to meet and form friendships with people you admire. Personal favorite: Raheem Sterling.

There's no question, the places I've traveled to are the highlight of my DP Bucket List. The French Riviera. London. Rio in Brazil. Even a zero-gravity space flight.

This job has basically allowed us to continually check boxes off of a bucket list that we honestly didn't even know we had.

CHALLENGE!

WHAT ABOUT YOU? Do you have a bucket list? If not, it's time to make one. Let your mind go wild! Dream big! Here are some helpful tips on creating your very own bucket list and setting some super cool goals. Don't worry, you can change this list and add to it over the years. Don't forget to check things off as you go.

1. Finish this sentence: "One day I really want to . . ."

2. What's an activity you'd love to do? Do you want to attempt any world records in that category?

3. Where's a place you really want to visit?

4. Is there someone famous you want to meet? Someone you admire? A personal hero?

5. What is something amazing that you would love to create one day?

6. What are some out-of-the-ordinary things you'd like to do? Don't be afraid to get weird or think outside the box. Maybe you want to watch an elephant paint a picture with its trunk in Thailand or go to kung fu school. (Really though—these things are possible . . . and more!)

7. The list can be short or long. The main thing is to *THINK BIG* and have fun with it.

CHAPTER FOURTEEN

WORLD RECORDS

THERE'S SOMETHING SPECIAL ABOUT HOISTING THAT CERTIFICATE, that world record-bestowing piece of paper. At that moment—until someone comes along to break that record, which has happend to us—you are the best in the world at something. Now that something might be extremely unimportant, like breaking a certain number of pencils in a short period of time, but hey, a record is a record!

We broke our first world record while filming our show. The pencil record was the very first! When we experienced the rush of breaking that record, we were hooked. So, we decided to try for more. Since then, we've done an entire basketball world record video as well as a football one. We've also broken hilarious records on our Overtime segment "Absurd Recurds." (Yes, it's spelled wrong on purpose—so that it rhymes, of course.) Going for a world record can be extremely challenging, but as you can imagine, the feeling of achieving one is pretty epic!

In 2009 Dude Perfect set the world record for the longest basketball shot after shooting from the fourth deck of Kyle Field at Texas A&M University. In October 2010, we extended our record with a "cross-tower" shot, which was 216 feet high, with the basket being 150 feet away from the tower's base. In March 2011, DP made a shot from the top of NRG Stadium in Houston, which lasted 5.3 seconds—but we didn't have a record official on hand, so it wasn't official. It technically only counts when it's verified by a judge or adjudicator. In January 2014, we successfully attempted a shot from the 561-foot-high Reunion Tower in downtown Dallas with Cody and Garrett holding the basket at the base of the tower. On May 11, 2016, we uploaded our "World Record Edition" where we broke twelve world records—eleven of them in basketball. A judge joined us, making it official.

TOTAL DUDE PERFECT INDIVIDUAL WORLD RECORDS (SO FAR)

PLAYER	RECORDS
	14
	9
	8
	7
	4

FUN FACT

In 2018 Dude Perfect broke the record for the farthest distance walking barefoot on LEGO bricks and farthest distance to blow a pea in "Overtime" episodes 2 and 3. In episode 6 of "Overtime," Dude Perfect broke the record for farthest distance traveled rolling on exercise balls. What's next? *STAY TUNED!*

"WORLD RECORD EDITION"

"World Record Edition" was a blast! A lot of our records have since been challenged and beaten, but here's a list of some things we were able to accomplish with practice and determination—and lots of teamwork.

Farthest basketball shot made with the head	TY, 37.125 FEET
Farthest blindfolded basketball hook shot	GARRETT, 55 FEET
Farthest basketball hook shot	TY, 70 FEET
Most basketball free throws in one minute by a pair (male)	COBY AND CORY, 35 FREE THROWS
Farthest basketball shot made while sitting on the court	CODY, 55.08 FEET
Farthest basketball bounce shot	CORY, 91 FEET 2 INCHES
Farthest behind-the-back basketball shot	CODY, 35.83 FEET
Farthest trampette basketball shot performing a forward flip	TY, 72 FEET
Most basketball three-pointers made by a pair in one minute	COBY AND CODY, 19 THREE-POINTERS
Longest basketball shot blindfolded	CODY, 71 FEET
Greatest height from which a basketball is shot	TY, 533 FEET

"WORLD RECORD EDITION 2"

We had so much fun with "World Record Edition," we had to make another one with football—"World Record Edition 2"— and this time, we earned twelve versus our previous eleven records. We're always looking to reach higher and farther to achieve our goals! Like our basketball records, some of our football records have since been challenged and beaten, but here's a look at what we accomplished.

Farthest American football throw into a target	TY, 50 YARDS
Farthest American field goal kick into a target	GARRETT, 30 YARDS
Most consecutive punt return catches caught and held	CODY, 5 FOOTBALLS
Longest American football pass caught between the legs (team of two)	TY, 35 YARDS
Farthest distance to hit a moving target with an American football throw	CODY, 30 YARDS
Most American football passes through a tire in one minute	TY, 37 THROWS
Most one-handed catches of an American football in one minute	TY, 42 CATCHES
Farthest catch of an American football while in motion	CORY, 22.3 YARDS
Longest behind-the-back catch of an American football	GARRETT, 41.3 YARDS
Longest pass of an American football through a tire	CODY, 30 YARDS
Greatest height from which an American football is thrown into a target	TY, 99.8 FEET
Greatest height from which an American football is caught	TY, 563 FEET

· CHAPTER FIFTEEN ·

OVERTIME

FOR YEARS, WE HAD THE IDEA of a variety show floating around in our heads. We had various segment ideas that we thought would make great videos, but they didn't necessarily fit into the category of a trick shot or battle. So, we finally got up the courage to launch a brand-new type of video, one where we could do almost anything—as long as it was extremely fun. Get Crafty, Wheel Unfortunate, Guess This Win That, Cool Not Cool, Betcha, Judge Dudy—you just never know what we'll come up with next.

On January 8, 2018, *Overtime* was born. Since then, "Overtime Episode 1" has been viewed more than 58 million times!

Here are some of our favorite *Overtime* segments that will hopefully encourage you to get creative and have fun!

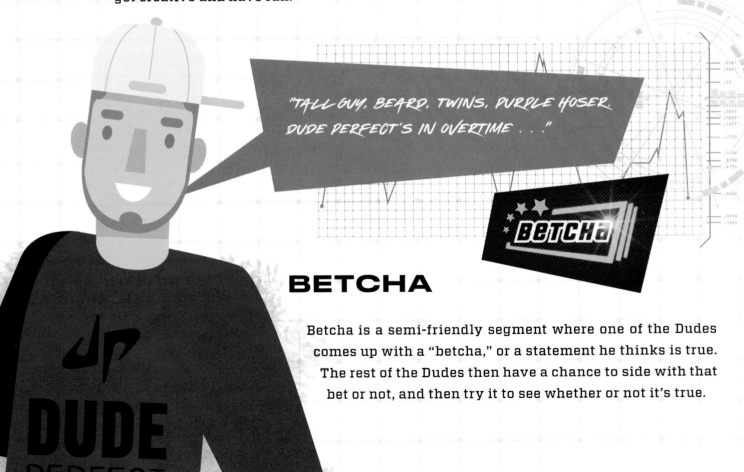

"TALL GUY, BEARD, TWINS, PURPLE HOSER.
DUDE PERFECT'S IN OVERTIME . . ."

BETCHA

Betcha is a semi-friendly segment where one of the Dudes comes up with a "betcha," or a statement he thinks is true. The rest of the Dudes then have a chance to side with that bet or not, and then try it to see whether or not it's true.

EPISODE 1:

In the first betcha, Tyler bet that it was possible to crush a diamond with a hammer. Tyler, Garrett, and Coby thought it possible, and they called their team the Shatter Train. Cody and Cory thought it was impossible and named their team Team Necklace—as in, the diamond is going to be in such perfect shape that they can make a necklace out of it.

RESULT:
The hammer was not able to break the diamond. The betcha was impossible, and Cody and Cory won.

EPISODE 3:

Tyler's betcha was that a car horn would not run out even after holding it down for thirty consecutive minutes. Everyone except Garrett thought it would go the distance. They then used a pickup truck and the horn beeped for only one minute exactly. Then they tried a car.

RESULT:
The car horn honked for thirty-one minutes straight. The beep seemed to stop, but everyone wasn't sure, because there was a slight sound. Then thirty seconds later it stopped entirely. Garrett tested the car, and it could still honk. So, everyone was officially confused and received a win that day.

EPISODE 6:

Cody bet he could swim a mile. Everyone except Cody thought he couldn't swim the distance. They went to the lake and took a boat one mile out from shore. Cody jumped into the water and swam toward shore while the rest of the guys followed along in a boat.

RESULT:

Amazingly, Cody swam the entire mile and made it to shore. Only Cody won that day.

EPISODE 10:

Cody bet he could sneak five hot dog wieners—in a row—into people's pockets, purses, and so on, without them realizing. Everybody except Garrett and Cory thought he could. Cody upped the ante and said that the last hot dog would be a foot-long.

RESULT:

After a couple of failed attempts, Cody managed to get five in a row: he successfully placed one in a stranger's cowboy boot, one in a box someone was carrying, one in a tool organizer on a belt, one in a stranger's back pocket, and—for the ultimate—a foot-long on a backpack.

EPISODE 17:

Tyler and Coby, as a dynamic duo, bet that an entire room full of cotton candy would fit into a drinking glass half-filled with water.

RESULT:

It started out great! And then . . . not so much. Ty jumped ship halfway through and avoided the dreaded consequences. The water turned a murky brown, and Coby tried to ball up the cotton candy to see if the compression would help. (It didn't.) Ty disowned Coby, and Coby lost his betcha.

BETCHAS OVERALL

NAME	WINS	LOSSES
CODY	4	1
CORY	2	3
TYLER	3	2
COBY	3	2
GARRETT	1	4

DID YOU KNOW?

It takes more than just the five of us Dudes to make these videos. Here's a little peek into the other important people and roles that make the magic happen. We love our always-expanding team!

4 VIDEO EDITORS: Our videos would be baaaad without them. Follow them @DPeditors.

1 SOCIAL MEDIA MASTERMIND AND PHOTOGRAPHER: Otherwise, our photos would look like they were taken with a potato.

1 CREATIVE ARTS DEPARTMENT GURU: You thought we built the *Overtime* set? That's very kind. Also, very untrue.

1 BUSINESS MANAGER: Being in business is better than being out of business.

1 LAWYER EXTRAORDINAIRE: We didn't have time for law school.

1 LOGISTICS GENIUS: Things are much more complex than they seem on the surface.

5 SCRUBBY DUDES who proudly dress like they're fourteen years old.

WHEEL UNFORTUNATE

"The Greatest Game Show of All Time!"

An *Overtime* special guest, the great Golden Boy Ned Forrester hosts Wheel Unfortunate. It's pretty simple: In this segment, the name of one of the guys is drawn from a hat. Whoever's name is drawn spins the wheel and has to do an unfortunate punishment.

There are exceptions though. In episode 12, the random draw didn't happen. That's because Coby went over the budget in Cool Not Cool ("Overtime 11") and then talked in the next episode, so he was automatically penalized into being the unfortunate participant.

In "Overtime 10," Ned was called to an emergency and called in his cohost, "Mr. Full Send," Jerry Senderson. Episode 6 was the only episode to not feature this segment. And episode 13 was the first time a DP video editor was selected as an unfortunate contestant. Who's been the most unfortunate so far? Let's take a look.

"CORY'S UNFORTUNATE *ALL THE TIME.*"
—NED FORRESTER

NED FORRESTER
"THE GOLDEN BOY" & HOST OF WHEEL UNFORTUNATE

"THIS IS THE WORST GAME SHOW IN THE WORLD."
—CORY COTTON

JERRY SENDERSON
"MR. FULL SEND" & BACKUP HOST OF WHEEL UNFORTUNATE"

THE UNFORTUNATE "WINNERS"

EPISODE	CONTESTANT	PUNISHMENT
1	CODY	Get a level 10 spray tan
2	CORY	Drive through a car wash on the windshield
3	CORY	Eat an entire banana—peel and all!
4	CORY	Fly to Wisconsin for no reason
5	GARRETT	Run a mile as a mascot
6	CORY	Shave your eyebrows
7	COBY	Get French Toasted
8	COBY	Sit in a box filled with snakes
9	TYLER	Milk a cow straight into your mouth
10	GARRETT	Stand in line at a theme park without riding any rides
11	COBY	Drive until you run out of gas
12	WILL (DP EDITOR)	Go on a date with a cardboard cutout
13	CORY	Wax your pits
14	CORY	Eat dog food out of a bowl like cereal
15	COBY	Shave your head
16	GARRETT	Spend a day as Gene Simmons
17	CORY	Sleep in a sandy bed

WHO'S *WHEELY* UNFORTUNATE?

There's been a clear unfortunate player on this segment since we started and that's none other than Cory. Not only has he consistently been randomly selected as a contestant, but he's picked his own name out of the hat five times! In segment fifteen, he channeled the Rage Monster and nearly flipped a table when he chose his own name—again!

NAME	OCCASIONALLY UNLUCKY.....................COMPLETELY UNFORTUNATE							
CORY	X	X	X	X	X	X	X	
COBY	X	X	X	X				
GARRETT	X	X						
CODY	X							
TYLER	X							
WILL (DP EDITOR)	X							

TASTE TESTS

In this segment, one of the guys is blindfolded and has to taste food and *blindly* label or rate it.

EPISODE 6

The guys blindfolded Garrett and had him try five different types of coffee. Garrett thought his order was (from best to worst) pour-over, Starbucks, fast food, instant coffee, and gas station coffee. However, Garrett's favorite coffee was actually the gas station coffee.

EPISODE 7

Tyler was blindfolded and tasted five different burgers from Burger King, In-n-Out, McDonald's, Wendy's, and Whataburger. He identified all of them except Wendy's and In-n-Out, which he swapped. Unlike Garrett, Tyler didn't have to rate the burgers from best to worst.

EPISODE 16

Cody was blindfolded and given the task of telling different pizzas apart from different restaurants. He was able to get all of them right, being the first person to get a perfect score in this segment, and earning the unofficial title "King of Pizza."

CHALLENGE!

Get a group of friends together and make your own taste test. Try different sodas, ice creams, or chicken fingers. Or throw a pizza party taste test. It's much harder than you might think! Don't forget the blindfolds!

ABSURD RECURDS

In Absurd Recurds, one of the guys will attempt to break a really absurd world record. An official judge regularly appears in this segment to make it official if the attempt succeeds.

IN EPISODE 2, Tyler completed a 146.94-foot LEGO walk barefoot.

IN EPISODE 3, Coby blew a pea 8.8 meters (28 feet, 10.5 inches!) across the floor in one breath.

IN EPISODE 6, Tyler traveled 290 feet across exercise balls.

IN EPISODE 9, Coby caught twenty-one Ping-Pong balls in his shaving cream-covered head.

IN EPISODE 11, Coby stacked seven donuts in one minute while being blindfolded.

IN EPISODE 12, Tyler opened fifty-two cans with one hand in sixty seconds.

IN EPISODE 15, Garrett and Cory did sixty-one headers with a beach ball in thirty seconds.

BOTTOM LINE:
TYLER AND COBY ARE CRUSHING IT AT BEING ABSURD!

CHALLENGE!

What absurd recurd do you want to try and break? Go for it!

COOL NOT COOL

In this segment of *Overtime*, each of the guys finds and buys an item they think is cool. Like a slightly more advanced show-and-tell, each Dude pitches his item, and then everyone votes whether they think it's cool or not cool.

So far, Cool Not Cool has made fourteen appearances. Episode 15 was the first time someone received a Super Not Cool—yes, that's right, zero cools—that being Cory. In fact, suspension was threatened if he didn't get a majority of cool votes in the next episode. What happened? Well, if you watched the episode, you know this didn't end well: Cory ended up being suspended from participating with a whopping four Not Cools.

Who has the most Cool item ratings? So far, that honor goes to Garrett Hilbert. He is also the only person who hasn't obtained an overall Not Cool score.

DUDE COOL FACTOR

We've gone through our voting history and—look—the numbers don't lie. Clearly, Garrett knows what items are cool. And Cory? Not so much.

NAME	SUPER NOT COOL	NOT COOL	COOL	SUPER COOL	PERCENT COOL ITEMS
GARRETT	0	0	11	4	100%
TYLER	1	1	9	4	86.67%
COBY	0	3	10	1	78.57%
CODY	0	4	6	5	73.33%
CORY	1	6	4	3	50%

THE COOL, THE NOT COOL, AND THE SUPER COOL

We love to show off items we find that we truly think are amazing and seriously cool. If everybody considers the item cool, then it will forever be designated as Super Cool. Four Cool votes is good, but it means it's almost Super Cool.

Here is the best of the best, the greatest of the great, the ultimate of the, er, ult? Anyway, here are our top ten favorite Super Cool items.

SUPER COOL FAVORITES

- PANCAKE MAKER
- CHOCOLATE GRENADES
- NET GUN
- UNSPILLABLE CUP
- WORLD'S STRONGEST LASER
- AIR CANNON
- 3-D PRINTER
- HOVER SHOES
- GRAPPLING GUN
- GIANT FLAMINGO

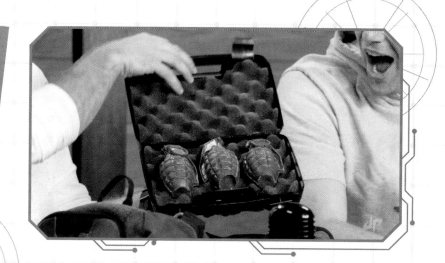

ANALYSIS

BEST PLAYER:

GARRETT. He has the highest percentage of Cool votes (83.5 percent). He has the highest percentage of getting his item certified Cool by the group (100 percent). He also is tied for the most Super Cools at four. It's not even close on this one.

WORST PLAYER:

CORY. He has the lowest percentage of Cool votes (60.77 percent). He has the lowest percentage of his item getting certified Cool by the group (53.85 percent). He does have three Super Cools, which puts him comfortably above Coby with only one Super Cool. We'll see if Cory can improve his score in the future!

TOUGHEST PLAYER TO GET A COOL FROM:

CODY only gives out 63.28 percent Cool votes.

MOST SUPER COOLS:

GARRETT, TYLER, AND CODY are all tied at the most with four Super Cools.

LEAST SUPER COOLS:

COBY with only one.

EASIEST PLAYER TO GET A COOL VOTE FROM:

COBY at an astonishing 75.83 percent. A full 4 percentage points higher than second-place Garrett.

MOST POWERFUL LASER

AIR CANNON

OVERTIME

NET GUN

COOL

POSSIBLE BIASES

Cory gives Coby a green only 41.67% of the time. This is 5 percent fewer points than Cory voting on Tyler's items and Garrett voting on Cody's items, which are the next lowest rates of person vs. person voting.

The data does seem to show a bias of left side vs. right side of the table as the viewer sees it. Garrett, Coby, and Tyler sit on the left. And Cody and Cory sit on the right. The left side consistently shows higher voting for themselves than voting for the right side. On the right side, Cory also shows a big bias of voting for his own (Cody). However, Cody does not seem to share in this bias. He just votes low for everybody.

CHALLENGE!

Get a group of your own friends or family together for a Cool Not Cool segment of your own! Each player brings an item to share, kind of like Show and Tell. The item doesn't even have to be new. And here's a tip: no matter what it is, sell it! Hype it up! Be enthusiastic! Make it sound like the coolest thing ever and show them why you love it. You might just win the Super Cool award!

PRO TIP Enthusiasm goes a long way in life!

· CHAPTER SIXTEEN ·

DOUBLE OVERTIME

DOUBLE OVERTIME? That's right. We thought we'd throw in something special for our book and share some things that you might not know about us.

LIFETIME STATS FROM DUDE PERFECT

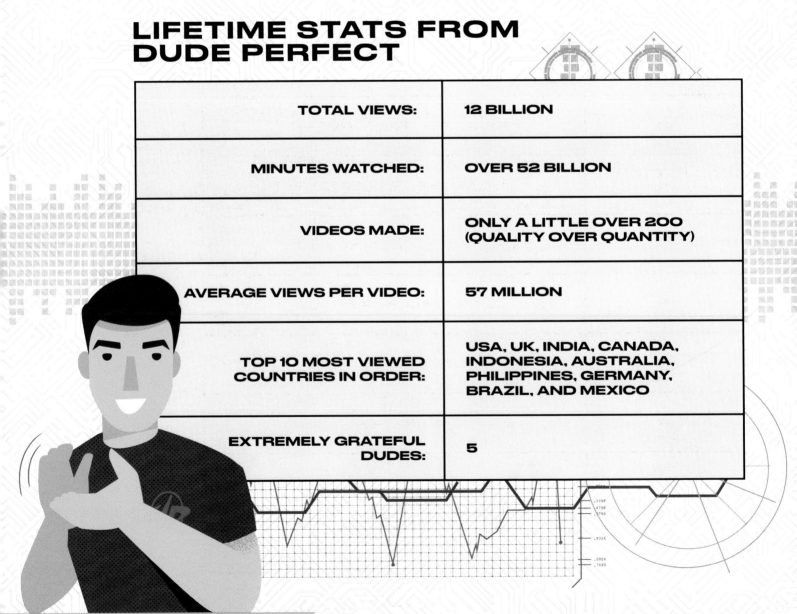

TOTAL VIEWS:	**12 BILLION**
MINUTES WATCHED:	**OVER 52 BILLION**
VIDEOS MADE:	**ONLY A LITTLE OVER 200 (QUALITY OVER QUANTITY)**
AVERAGE VIEWS PER VIDEO:	**57 MILLION**
TOP 10 MOST VIEWED COUNTRIES IN ORDER:	**USA, UK, INDIA, CANADA, INDONESIA, AUSTRALIA, PHILIPPINES, GERMANY, BRAZIL, AND MEXICO**
EXTREMELY GRATEFUL DUDES:	**5**

TOP TEN MOST POPULAR DP VIDEOS

We've made hundreds of videos over the years and it's fun to see our fans' reactions to our crazy ideas. Sometimes you surprise us! Like which videos are your absolute favorite. We were taking a look at the standings and thought you might find it as interesting as we do.

These are the top ten most-viewed Dude Perfect videos, in order of views. We would list the number of views, but it changes literally every day!

RANKING	VIDEO
1	WATER BOTTLE FLIP 2
2	PING-PONG TRICK SHOTS 3
3	REAL LIFE TRICK SHOTS 2
4	REAL LIFE TRICK SHOTS
5	PING-PONG TRICK SHOTS 2
6	AIRPLANE TRICK SHOTS
7	BEACH STEREOTYPES
8	RC EDITION
9	FLIP EDITION
10	FIDGET SPINNER TRICK SHOTS

CELEBRATIONS

If you haven't figured it out by now, we are all about having fun and celebrating life. Each day is a gift and a cause for celebration on its own. And when you add a victory or a win on top of that it deserves a bonus celebration!

Here are some of our favorite celebratory moves and catchphrases.

"YES!" A trusted favorite. Because yes is so much better than no.

"YEAH!" A more excited version of "Yes."

"WHHOOOOOHHH!" Pure squealing delight.

"WOO-HOO!" This is Texan for "Whooh!"

"BWAHAHAHAHAHA!" The delirious laugh, because what just happened was insane.

"WHOA!" Did that really just happen? Unbelievable, because that was awesome.

"AGGHHHHHH!!!" A howling scream to frighten your neighbors.

"BANG!" Especially good when you make a tough shot.

"LET'S GO!" Best said while running with your arms out like an airplane.

"ARE YOU KIDDING ME?" Say it in ALL CAPS. Not "are you kidding me" or even "Are You Kidding Me?" No. ALL CAP IT, BABY.

"YEEEEEEEEAAAAAAAHHHHHHHH!" The scream with the popping vein in the forehead. Terrifying. Watch out.

"GOT IT." Straightforward, reminding everybody you actually *did* get the shot.

And of course, the celebratory catchphrases can often be accompanied by celebratory actions. In fact, they probably should be. Otherwise, it might get weird.

THE VICTORY RUN.
Dedicated. Focused.

THE PRE-CLAP.
Clapping hands before screaming out "Yeah!"

HIGH FIVE.
The universal acknowledgment for just about anything.

THE BEAR HUG.
Friends forever. Often used after a successful trust shot.

THE FIST PUMP.
Cool, collected.

THE CHEST BUMP.
Sometimes, it's a side bump. Jumping is often involved.

DEADPAN.
No word, no motion. Just soak in the moment.

TOUCHDOWN.
No footballs necessary.

ARMS OUTSTRETCHED,
Let's gooooo!

THE BOW.
Courteous, professional, humble.

THE STORY OF A BEAR

We wanted to take a moment to give Panda proper credit for all the joy he's brought to the team. If you don't know by now who Panda is, he's our amazing mascot. But he's so much more than that. As for how he came to be part of our team, well . . .

Out on a drive one night at the ranch, Cody saw something in the trees.

It was big.

It was black and white.

It was masked.

What was a panda doing in Texas?

We didn't know, but we set out to catch it and find out. After several failed attempts, we hit on the perfect trap: popcorn!

Once we caught him, we decided to show him what we do. And it turns out that Panda was a natural at fiery trick shots, dunks, and high fives—except when hanging from a tree branch was involved. He's been part of Dude Perfect ever since, and he's the best mascot ever. (But really, who chose whom?)

How to keep a Panda happy? Don't run out of popcorn!

ANATOMY OF PANDA

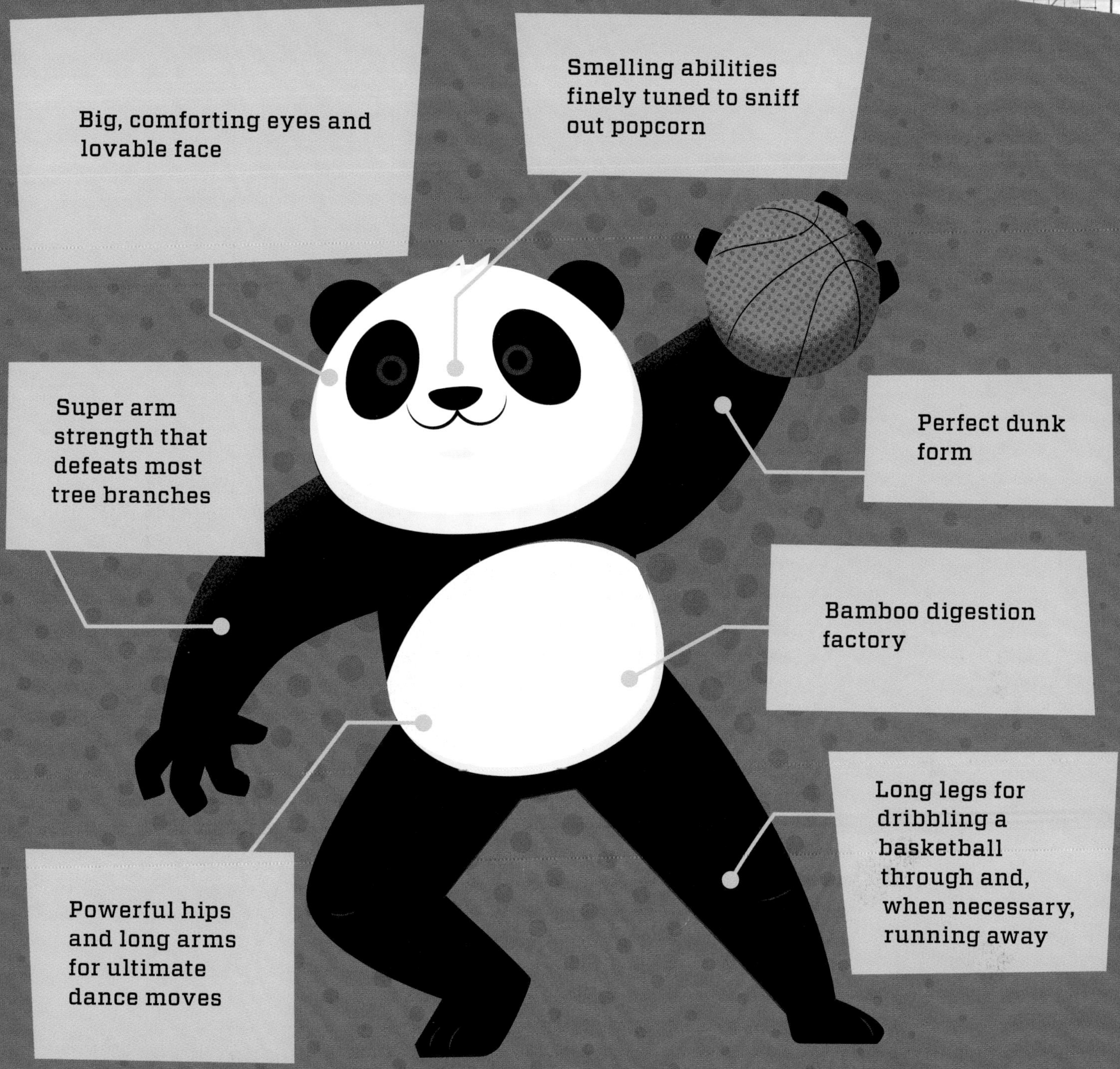

Big, comforting eyes and lovable face
Smelling abilities finely tuned to sniff out popcorn
Super arm strength that defeats most tree branches
Perfect dunk form
Bamboo digestion factory
Long legs for dribbling a basketball through and, when necessary, running away
Powerful hips and long arms for ultimate dance moves

TEN TERRIFIC *PANDA* MOMENTS

He is a mammal of mystery. A beast with a little-known backstory. A creature who makes everyone curious.

Who *is* Panda?

While we can't give that away just yet (or probably ever), we can share some stu**panda**eous moments with Panda. Some **panda**wesome appearances he makes in our videos. Fan**panda**tastic cameos made by the animal himself. (Did you know that you can add the word "panda" to any amazing word you can think of? Okay . . . you can't, but that didn't stop us from trying!)

1. ***The Panda Trust Shot***
    It doesn't always go well (like when Tyler tried to knock an apple off Panda's head), but boy is it funny.

2. ***Runaway Panda***
    When we were trying to catch Panda, Ty tried getting him with a fake tranquilizer dart, but Panda somehow managed to run away.

3. ***Bear Tackle***
    Panda gets full-form tackled in our "NFL Kicking Edition" video. His head comes off. Just saying.

4. **Skateboarding Bear**

Check out our "Epic Trick Shot Battle 2" to see one of Panda's most epic trick shots ever . . . on a skateboard!

5. **The Come-from-Behind Out-of-Nowhere Victory**

Was there ever a question that Panda would win the Go-Kart Battle? All he needed to do was avoid the crash at turn five to take the checkered flag!

6. **Sinking the Panda**

While playing Giant Warship Battle on Team Blue with Tyler and Garrett, Panda is three for three on his shots. Then he is sunk. Okay, maybe this was an almost-highlight for our beloved Panda.

7. **Adrift with Panda**

While the Dudes have fun on the "Nerf Blasters: Lake House Edition" video, Panda rides a WaveRunner, steers a sailboat, and chills in a canoe.

8. **Panda's Funniest Moment**

Every time Panda falls out of a tree . . . which is most times he tries to climb into a tree. You have to cut him some slack though; he's domesticated.

9. **Panda Edition**

Should we do an entire trick shot video featuring only Panda? Comment in our videos and let us know!

10. **"BREAKING NEWS: Dude Perfect Panda Reveal"**

For the last ten years, the biggest question we get is "Who is Panda?" We decided to make an offer: we will reveal his identity when we make it to number one on the most-subscribed spot for YouTube. As of today, the offer still stands, so let's go!

LIFE LESSONS FROM THE DUDES

Life's a funny thing. It's a combination of relationships, choices, results, and our response to those results. Whether you're making trick shots for a living or being the best student you can be, we've found that oftentimes, it's the simple things that help you go far in life. Here are some of our favorites, tips both big and small, that have made a difference for us. Some we've learned from our Christian faith, and some we've learned by making lots of mistakes. We wanted you to have them.

1. HAVE A FIRM HANDSHAKE.

2. LOOK PEOPLE IN THE EYE.

3. LOVE EVERYONE. (TREAT PEOPLE—IN REAL LIFE AND ON SOCIAL MEDIA— THE WAY YOU WANT TO BE TREATED.)

4. OPEN DOORS FOR OTHER PEOPLE. (BE SELFLESS.)

5. KEEP YOUR NOSE DOWN WHEN YOU WIN AND YOUR HEAD UP WHEN YOU LOSE.

6. READ YOUR BIBLE.

7. CHOOSE GOOD FRIENDS.

8. CHOOSE GOOD FRIENDS. YES WE REPEATED IT. IT'S THAT IMPORTANT.

9. MAKE YOUR BED.

10. HUG YOUR PARENTS AND SIBLINGS. FAMILIES ARE IMPORTANT. LOVE AND TREAT THEM WELL.

11. IF YOU REALLY WANT TO BE AMAZING AT SOMETHING, YOU'RE GOING TO HAVE TO WORK *RIDICULOUSLY* HARD AT IT.

12. ASK OTHERS FOR HELP WHEN YOU NEED IT, BUT NEVER ASK ANYONE TO HELP YOU MOVE. YOU'RE A BETTER FRIEND THAN THAT.

13. REMEMBER, EVERYONE YOU MEET IS BETTER THAN YOU AT SOMETHING.

14. DON'T TAKE THINGS TOO PERSONALLY OR TAKE LIFE TOO SERIOUSLY.

15. DON'T EVER—AND WE DO MEAN NEVER EVER—SHOOT A TRICK SHOT WITHOUT PRESSING RECORD.

A FINAL NOTE
FROM THE DUDES

Dude Perfect is as much fun as it looks. It's also a lot more work than it seems. But we're happy to do it in order to bring fun videos to people all across the world. We are incredibly honored that anyone wants to watch us five goofballs, and we have no plan of stopping this adventure! As always, we want you to know how thankful we are for you personally. Thank you for reading this book and for following along with all our craziness. Hopefully we'll meet you on the street one day or at one of our live shows. Until then, wherever you are, God bless! We'll leave you the only way we know how . . .

POUND IT
NOGGIN
SEE YA!

BIBLIOGRAPHY

Editors of Encyclopaedia Britannica. "Pyramids of Giza." *Encyclopaedia Brittanica*. Updated April 1, 2020. Accessed December 17, 2020. <https://www.britannica.com/topic/Pyramids-of-Giza#ref257548>

English, Trevor. "The Math behind Throwing the Perfect Football Spiral." Interesting Engineering. February 29, 2020. Accessed November 20, 2020. <interestingengineering.com/the-math-behind-throwing-the-perfect-football-spiral>

"Facts and Figures about Materials, Waste, and Recycling." United States Environmental Protection Agency. Updated September 10, 2020. Accessed December 15, 2020. <https://www.epa.gov/facts-and-figures-about-materials-waste-and-recycling/plastics-material-specific-data>

Harris, Tom. "How Water Slides Work." HowStuffWorks. August 31, 2001. Accessed November 14, 2020. <https://science.howstuffworks.com/engineering/structural/water-slide.htm>

"Playing with Waves." G&G. August 2011. Accessed November 9, 2020. <https://www.businesstoday.in/magazine/how-things-work/rc-toys-radiowaves/story/17649.html>

Science Buddies; Finio, Ben. "The Physics of Bottle Flipping." Bring Science Home. March 8, 2018. Accessed November 20, 2020. <https://www.scientificamerican.com/article/the-physics-of-bottle-flipping/>

Spector, Bennett. "The History and Evolution of the NERF Football." Bleacher Report. December 13, 2011. Accessed November 21, 2020. <https://bleacherreport.com/articles/974948-the-history-and-evolution-of-the-nerf-football-the-worlds-first-indoor-ball>

"Table Tennis." The International Olympic Committee. Accessed December 17, 2020. < https://www.olympic.org/seoul-1988/table-tennis>

ACKNOWLEDGMENTS

JESUS: Thank You for saving us. You are where our true hope and joy is found. We'd trade it all for You in an instant. That said, thank You for the opportunity of Dude Perfect. We're not sure why You chose us five, but our prayer is that we honor You with the platform You've given us and bless others in the process.

OUR WIVES: Just, wow. We are a mess, and unfortunately, you're stuck with us. Because of your love, you've allowed us to follow our dreams. Thank you for loving us and our kids so well. We are forever proud of you and thankful for you. God has been too good to us.

OUR PARENTS: Up until this point, you've put up with us the longest. Now that we have kids of our own, we *kind of* get it. Thank you for all the late nights, car rides, and priceless moments. We could not have asked for better parents. We are absurdly grateful, and we hope to repay you by allowing you to watch our cute kids while we go watch a movie. (JK.) But seriously—we promise to say thank you more often than we used to. Love you guys.

OUR SIBLINGS: Thank you for being our ride-or-die best friends through all of this. Y'all are way cooler than us. If you currently don't live near us, please move closer. And if you do live nearby, please move closer.

YOUTUBE: From the platform itself, to all the executives and team managers we've worked with along the way, thanks for giving us a way to do what we do, in all its uniqueness. You have been awesome to us, and we are genuinely thankful.

THE DP TEAM—

JEFF: Thank you for fathering Tyler (just feels like it needs to be said), and then for becoming a second father to the rest of us. Thank you for taking care of us and our business all these years and for consistently pushing us to see all that Dude Perfect can really become. You inspire us and we are unbelievably grateful for you.

EDITORS: You pour your hearts into your work to turn our loud and unwatchable footage into the extremely high-quality, slightly less loud, totally fun and enjoyable videos that people know and love. We are a video company at heart, and you make the videos so much more than we could on our own. Thanks for the arm-burning camera holding, the screen-glaring editing, the late nights, early mornings, endless video comments, and yes—even though we sometimes (often) give you a hard time for them—the Editor Editions.

SAM: Thanks for dotting the i's and crossing the t's. Thanks for protecting us and always having our best interest in mind. You are the man, and we appreciate you more than you know.

RYAN: Thanks for putting the team on your back (often literally) and for making sure our sets and physical builds are at a level of excellence that we can be immensely proud of. You consistently blow us away.

MARGARET: Thanks for taking care of all of the minutia that would literally never get done without you. Thanks for sticking by our side for so long. You have meant so much to this team, and we can't thank you enough.

HASH: You make us look good—or at least better—with all your nifty camera clicks. You've elevated our social game to a whole other level. There's no doubt about it—you've made Dude Perfect better and more fun all around. We're thrilled to have you.

SPARKY: Thank you for all the hilarious one-liners, the wizardry on the sticks, and for making DP gaming a thing. Thanks for cameo-ing in videos and for eating those horrible burgers we made for you. You are one of a kind. Don't ever change.

FANS: Lastly, thank you to each and every Dude Perfect fan. We're still blown away that you want to take this journey with us. We've got a million ideas and some really exciting plans. God willing, we'll be doing this for a long time. The best is yet to come!

ABOUT THE AUTHOR

A free sandwich, a simple camera, and twenty "I can do better than you" shots later, Dude Perfect was born. When that first ball swished, they had no idea what they were getting themselves into, but they believe that nothing happens by accident, that God has given them this platform for a reason, and that they have an opportunity to make an impact on the lives of countless others all around the globe. As a result, Cory Cotton, Coby Cotton, Garrett Hilbert, Cody Jones, and Tyler Toney—all of whom were former college roommates at Texas A&M University—have gone on to reach more than 12 billion viewers and hopefully the same number of smiles all around the globe.

For more about DudePerfect—and to see all of our videos—please visit DudePerfect.com or check out our Dude Perfect channel on YouTube.